# What on Earth is it?

*Fascinating and intriguing implements from yesteryear*

Illustrated by John Broadley

**Dalesman**

First published in 2005 by Dalesman
*an imprint of*
Country Publications Ltd
The Water Mill
Broughton Hall
Skipton
North Yorkshire
BD23 3AG

First edition 2005



ISBN 1 85568 225 7



Repro by PPS Grasmere, Leeds
Printed by Compass Press

# Introduction

They're in our attics, cellars and barns; they turn up at car-boot sales and auction rooms, and most of us are just left uttering 'What on earth…?'

They're the strange and intriguing implements that were once part of daily life, now replaced by some piece of technological wizardry or time-saving device.

Since 1994 *Dalesman* magazine has been testing its readers' memories and ingenuity with a monthly column featuring these weird and wonderful objects, painstakingly and accurately drawn by John Broadley. Now we bring together the best of them in one book for you to test your wits and recollections. Thankfully, the answers are in the back.

We are indebted to all who contributed objects and, of course, to those who supplied the solutions.

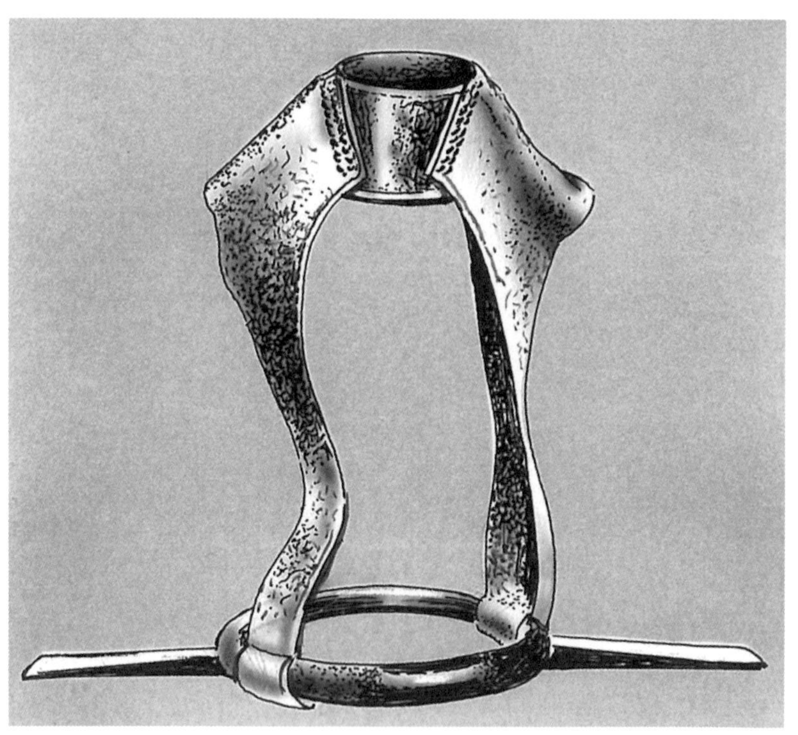

This baffling contraption consists of a leather harness or collar attached to a heavy metal ring, with two flat metal handles projecting three inches either side of the ring. The sturdy leather harness has heavy panels on either side which lead to an equally robust collar with a one and a half inch diameter hole. But what on earth was it for?

*answer on page 76*

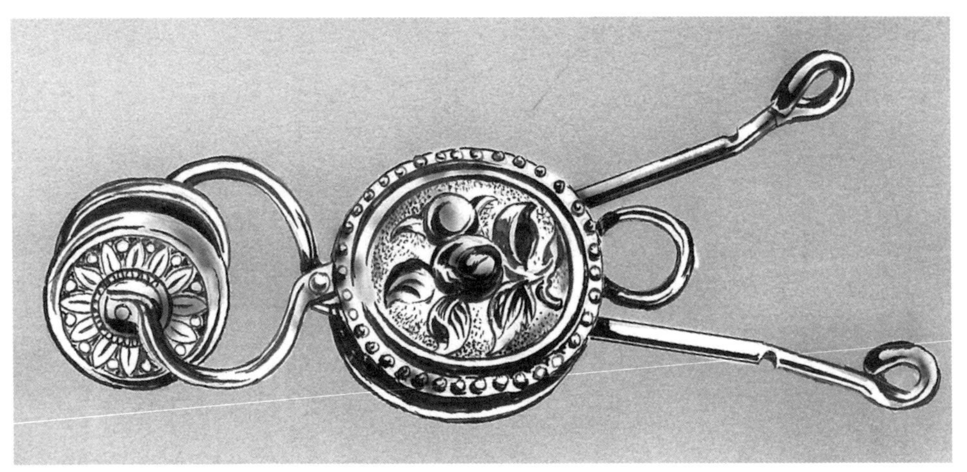

Now here is a dainty puzzle: a very delicate and ornate conundrum, perhaps made of silver though there is no marking, and with some fine decoration. Five inches long, it consists of two discs, padded with cork, which can be clipped firmly together or snapped apart by sliding the central disc up and down. At the top are three loops. All very lovely. But what on earth is it?

*answer on page 76*

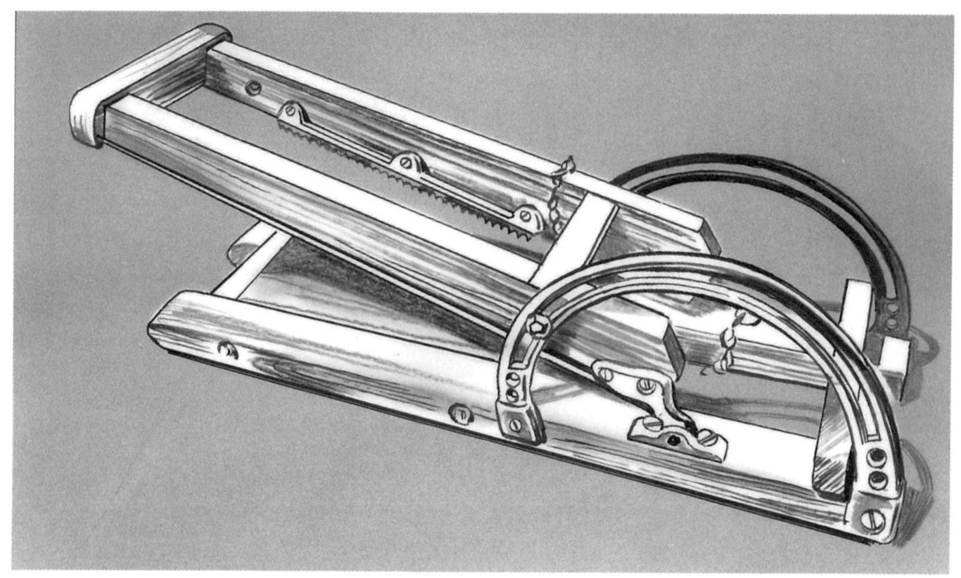

At first glance, this might be one of those primitive but effective catapults that knights of old were wont to use to lob boulders into the castles of those who offended them. But it would be only a small boulder from this contraption, which measures just two feet long. It is nevertheless a sturdy piece of equipment on a heavy wooden base with a brace of equally hefty hinged spars. These can be raised or lowered and then locked into place with bolts that run on a semicircular iron frame on either side. Just to add a final conundrum, the underside of the spars has a row of metal teeth. But what did they bite on?

*answer on page 76*

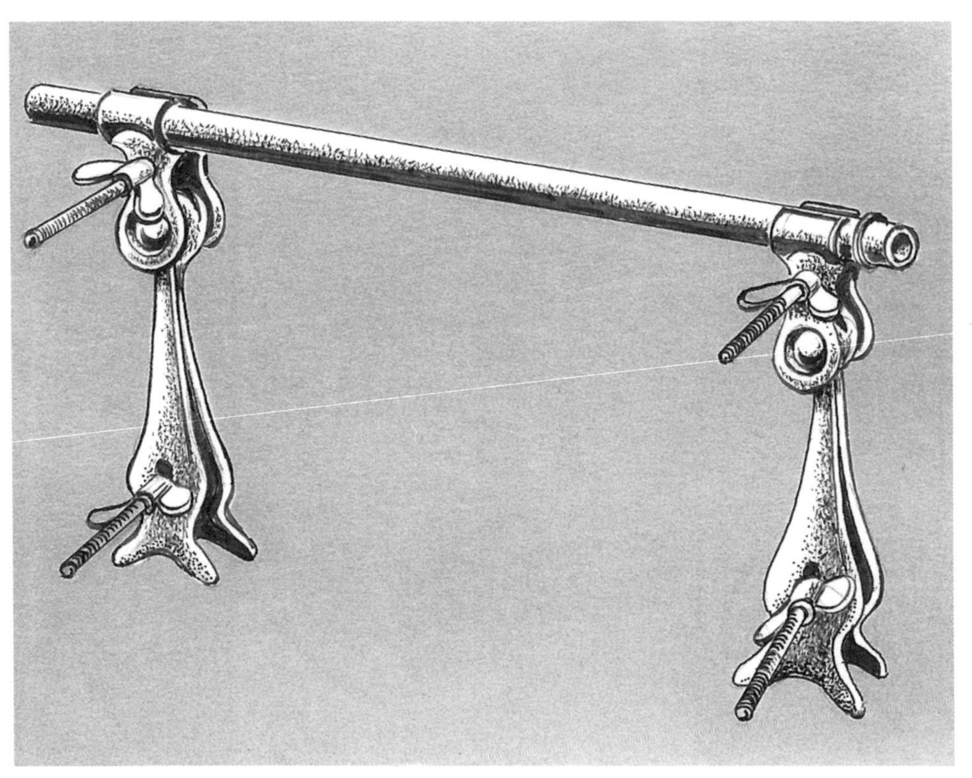

This rusted and pitted curiosity consists of two adjustable clamps attached to a hollow pipe. Each of the clamps has a ball joint for maximum flexibility and ends in another adjustable clamp. Its sturdy construction suggests it was used for tough work. But what?

*answer on page 76*

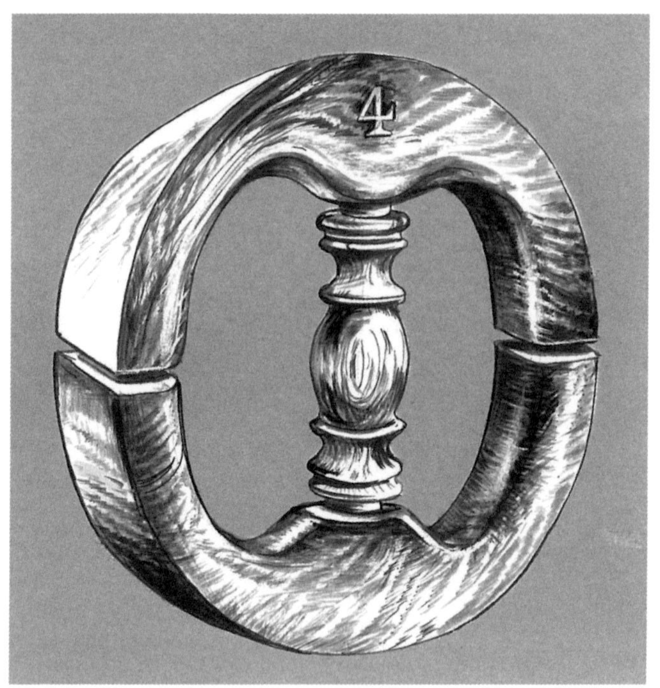


This rather splendid wooden device has obviously had plenty of use, worn smooth with handling and bearing the patina of considerable age. It has been skillfully made and lovingly cared for. The outer oval frame, just a hand's span across, has been carved with the figure 4, while the centre spindle turns to gently ease the two halves apart. Ingenious, but what on earth is it?

*answer on page 77*

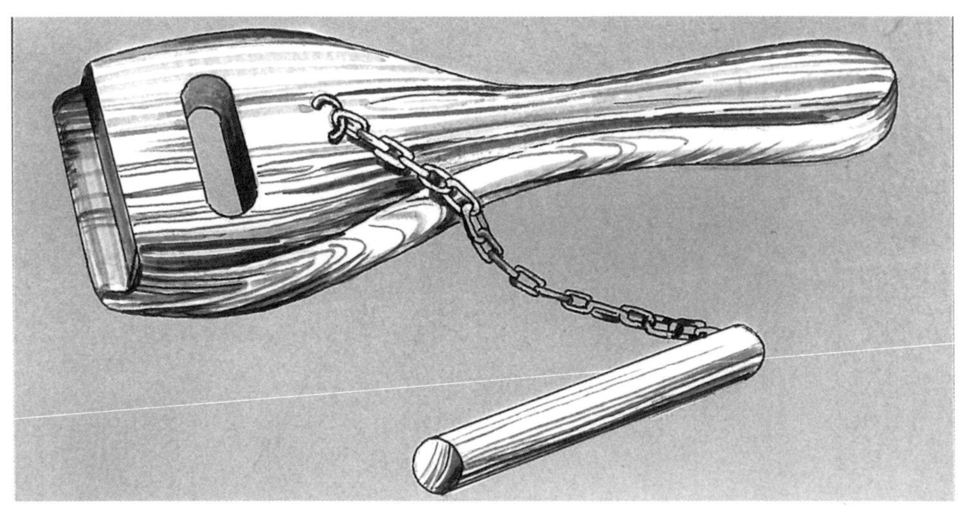

At first glance this peculiar device has a slightly homemade air about it. It was found in the tool kit of a man who made his living as a carpet fitter and upholsterer, but who was able to turn his hand to almost anything and so it could be for almost any purpose. It is a solid wooden paddle which measures a little over ten inches long by just over three inches at its widest. The wooden rod is four and a half inches long and three-quarters of an inch in diameter, and slips easily through the slot in the widest part of the paddle. The rod is attached by an eight-inch chain, which is firmly screwed to both pieces but is not particularly robust. The final clue is a just-off-square groove cut from the end of the paddle. What is it for?

*answer on page 77*

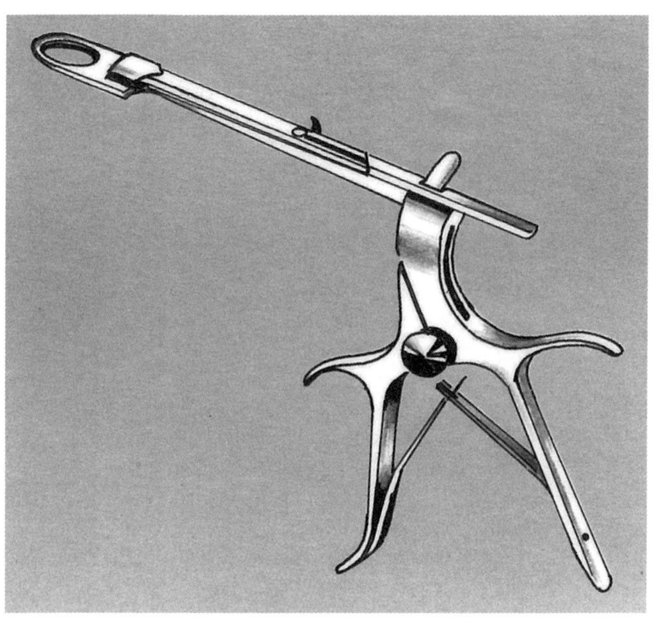

This intriguing mechanical device is stamped with the words 'Scholl LONDON' which may suggest something to do with foot treatment, but it also bears the words 'H M Government'. The device is roughly pistol-shaped with spring-loaded handles which can be squeezed together. This pushes a slider along the 'barrel' to partly cover the hole at the end. The end of the slider is blunt and has never been filed, so it is definitely not a cutter, and the slider does not completely cover the hole but leaves an eighth of an inch clearance. What was its use?

*answer on page 77*

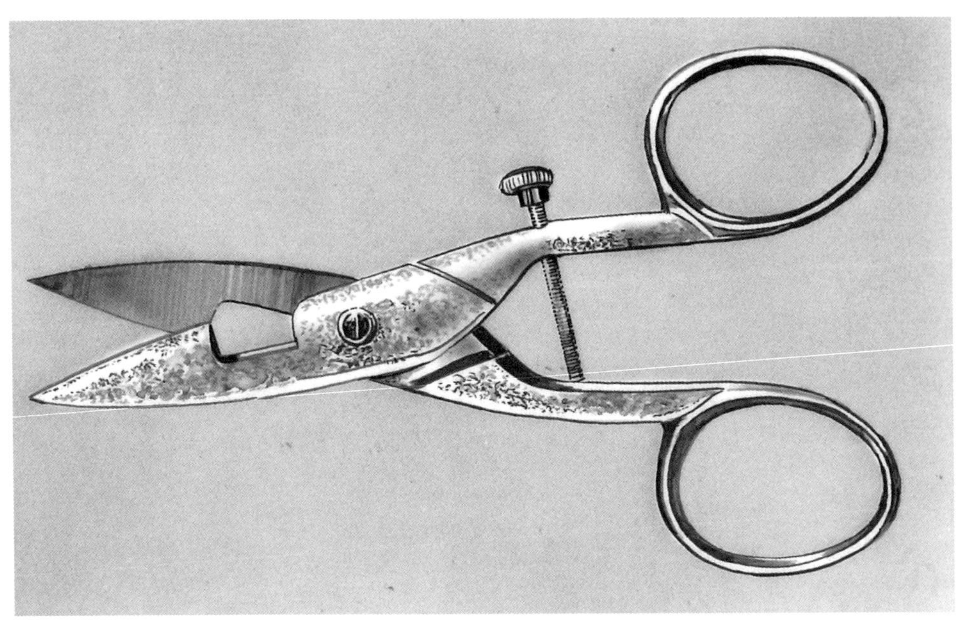

At first glance, this is just an ordinary pair of scissors. But take a closer look and it becomes clear this is no standard pair from the sewing basket. Inspection of the scissors, just four inches long, reveals two important modifications. Firstly, a finely threaded, one-inch-long screw has been drilled through one arm of the scissors, and this can be adjusted to either allow the blades to close completely or to be held partly open at a pre-set distance. Secondly, there is a half-inch-wide notch cut out of the blades. But why?

*answer on page 77*

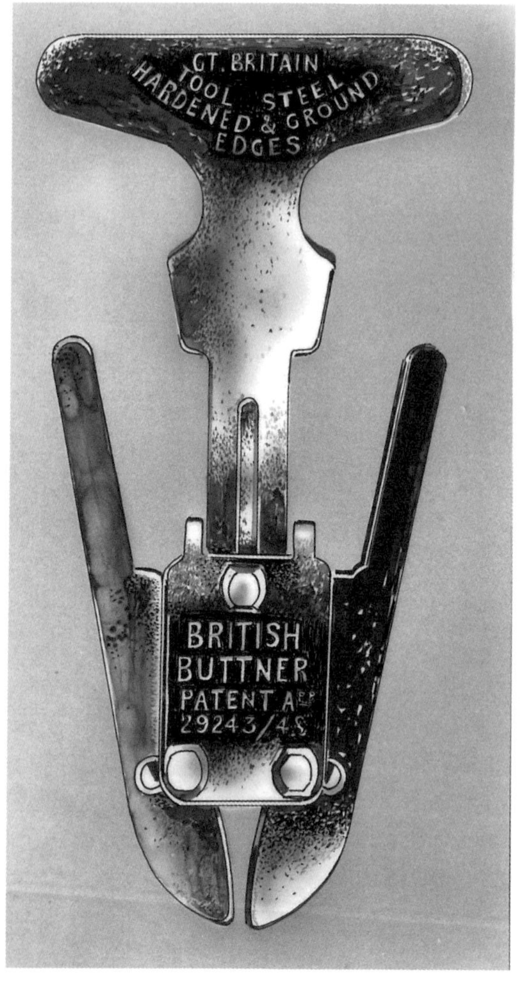


This object is quite small — just two and a half inches long — and made of hardened steel. The steel arms open and close easily, and there is no cutting edge. The device has a special protective leather case. Could it be a gauge of some kind. Or if not, what?

*answer on page 78*

This is a domestic utensil which could prompt some strange suggestions as to its use. The wooden and metal handle ends in two open but different-sized egg cup shapes. What on earth was it used for?

*answer on page 78*

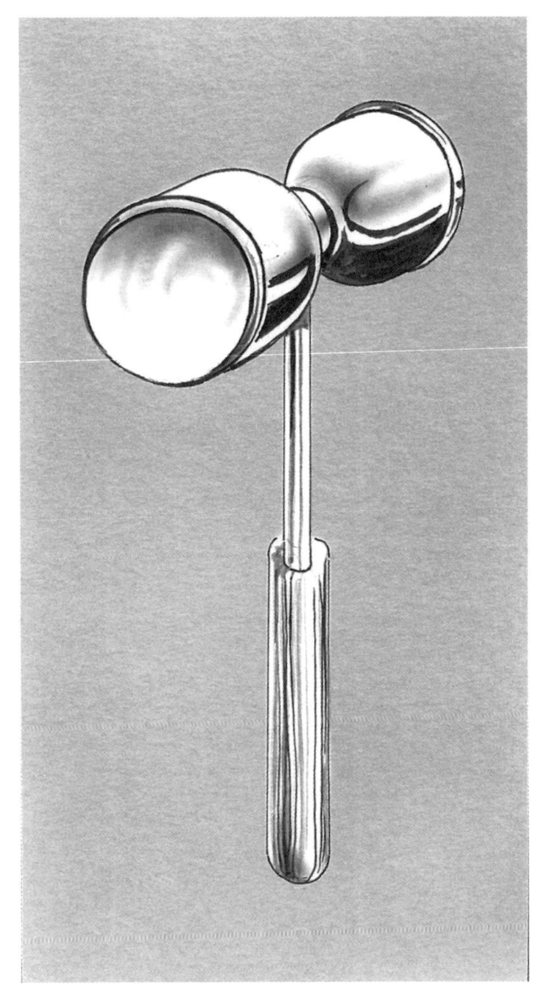

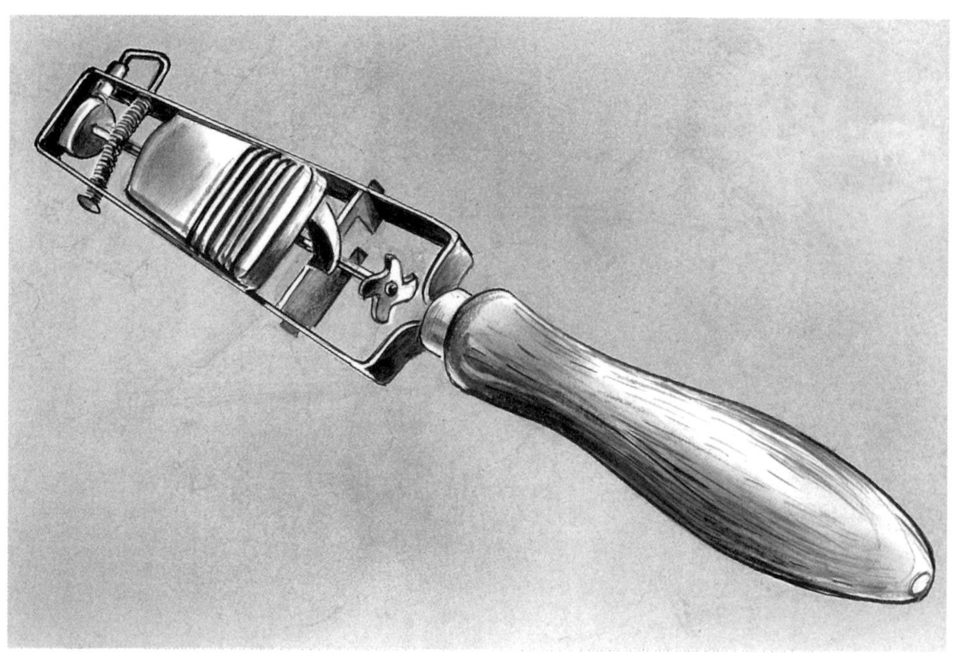

This gadget is ingenious and certainly quite old, with the wooden handle carrying the patina of long use. The mechanism is simple but ingenious. When holding the handle in the palm of the hand, the thumb can be used to press down on the broad, flat trigger, which in turn locks into a star-shaped wheel. The wheel then turns a spindle which is attached to another wheel at the far end and rubs it against a spring-loaded bar. Very clever — but what was it used for?

*answer on page 78*

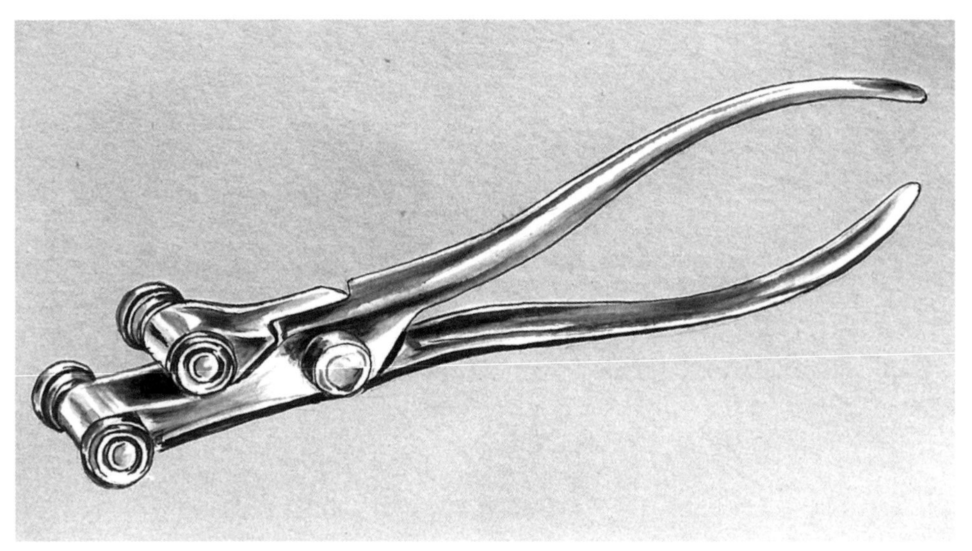

This item resembles a pair of pliers, but instead of grips it has a baffling set of offset rollers. When the handles are closed, the two heads — each of which has a free-turning roller at either end — are about an inch apart. When the handles are opened to the maximum range, the two heads are two inches apart. It is not possible to grip anything between the two heads, though it may be possible to stretch something open — but what?

*answer on page 78*

This handy device seems to be a cross between a Russian doll and a wooden puzzle. It measures just over three inches long by an inch in diameter, and divides into three sections. The 'nose cone' unscrews to reveal a central compartment holding the wooden spindle. This is also hollow with its own removable top. The bottom section also unscrews to reveal another small compartment. But what was it used for?

*answer on page 79*

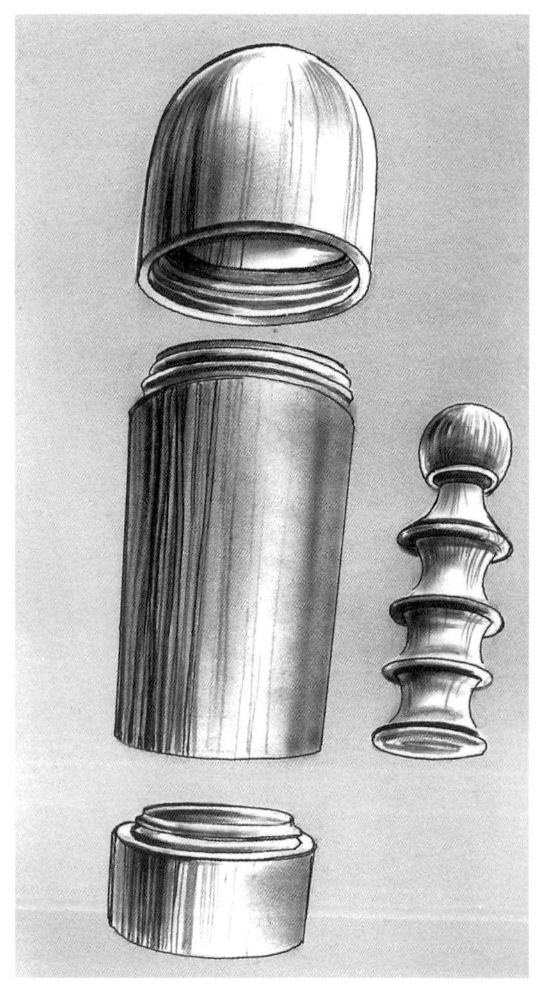

This intriguing object has a main section eight inches long, carved from wood and has a handle with a bulbous top, shaped rather like a baby's rattle. A groove has been cut into this, and into it fits a smaller stick, held in place by a plaited leather thong. The string acts like a spring, allowing the stick to be pressed back against the handle but spring back outwards to the position shown in the drawing. But what on earth was it?

*answer on page 79*

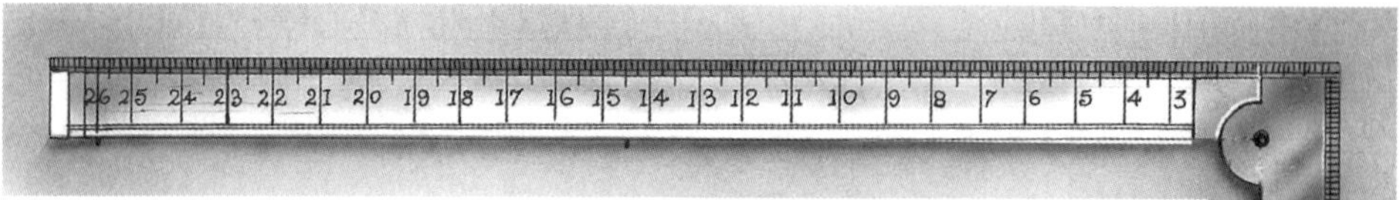

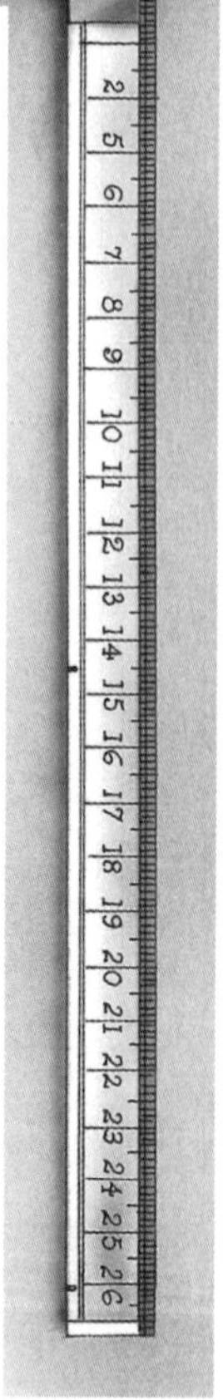

Sometimes items that at first glance seem simple to recognise can throw up the most subtle puzzles. Take this ruler, for example. At initial acquaintance, it seems a first cousin to those joiners' folding rulers that used to fascinate small boys allowed to rummage in dad's toolkit. But closer inspection reveals some unsuspected quirks. Most notably, it does not fold open completely straight because its brass hinge is designed to open only as far as a right angle. Then there is the odd length, twenty-seven inches. The front of the ruler is marked out in conventional feet and inches, but the reverse is divided by a very peculiar system. There is a mark for eighteen inches, but the other marks, for two-thirds, half and quarter, are all based from that, so that two-thirds is at twelve inches, half at nine inches and so on. Obviously it was designed for a special purpose. But what?

*answer on page 79*

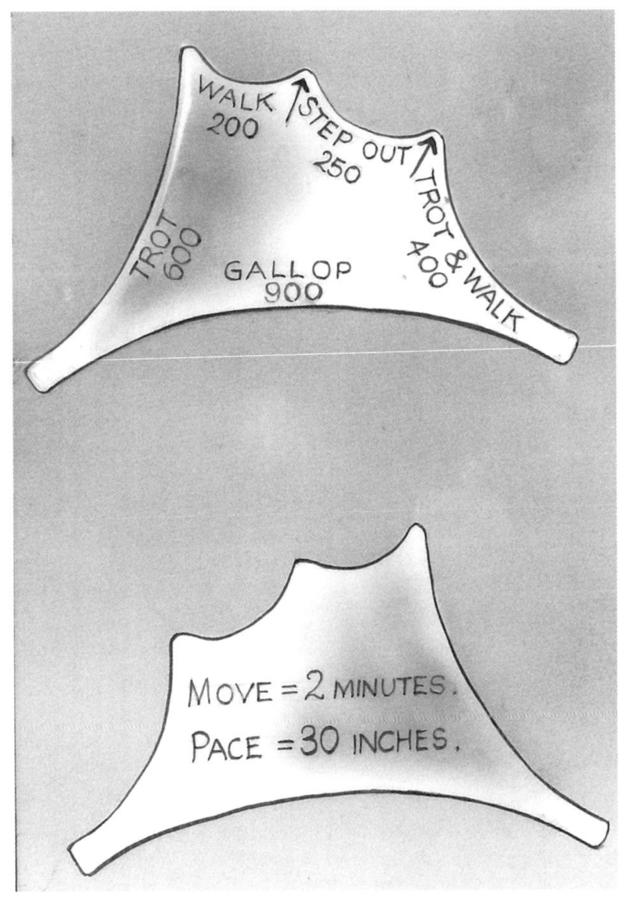


Made of brass and of a distinctly strange shape, this item obviously has horsey connections. The chief clues are in the markings, which suggests it may also have military links. The scoops along the sides carry different markings, the largest being 'Gallop 900', the next largest 'Trot 600', the next 'Trot and Walk 400', followed by 'Step out 250' and finally 'Walk 200'. On the reverse side is marked 'Move = 2 Minutes' and 'Pace = 30 inches'. What on earth was it for?

*answer on page 79*

Although it is only nine inches high, this sturdy little machine looks as though it means business. It has fourteen holes of various sizes up to an inch across in the base. The twelve smallest are numbered one to twelve, but the largest two are unmarked. The metal rod on the side stores nine tapering metal blocks, though the length of the rod suggests some of these may be missing. The machine itself is marked 'Pinfolds Patent'. It is clearly some kind of engineering tool. But what?

*answer on page 80*

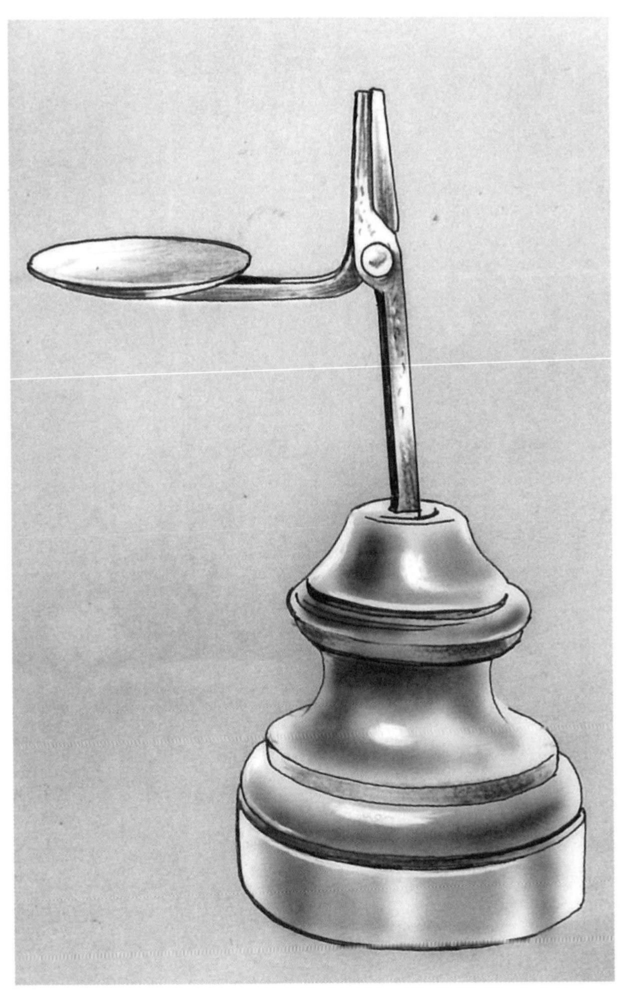

This item is clearly very old, its wooden base eaten by worms and its iron top pitted with rust. It stands a little under two feet high, and the sturdy base has the patina of years of polish, so it was probably a domestic rather than a workshop item. The metal upright ends in a pair of spring-loaded jaws, one arm of which has a circular dish to the side. What on earth was it used for?

*answer on page 80*

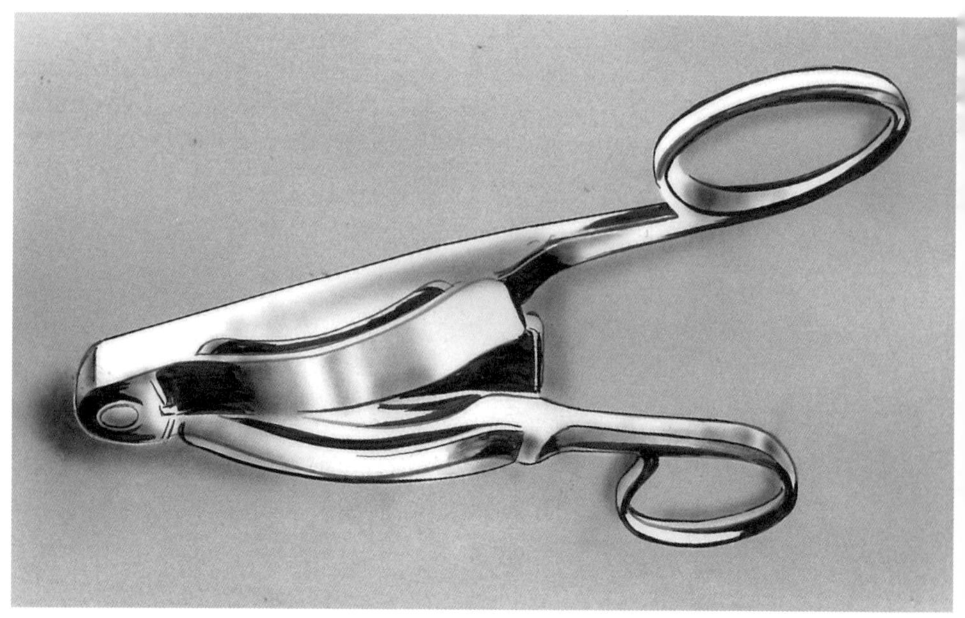

This handsome device is made of solid brass, and resembles a pair of nutcrackers in both size and construction. They open out to a full 180° and, like nutcrackers, have a hollow scooped out. But the bottom of the hollow is almost closed, with a toothed guard which slips over the slot. What on earth is it?

*answer on page 80*

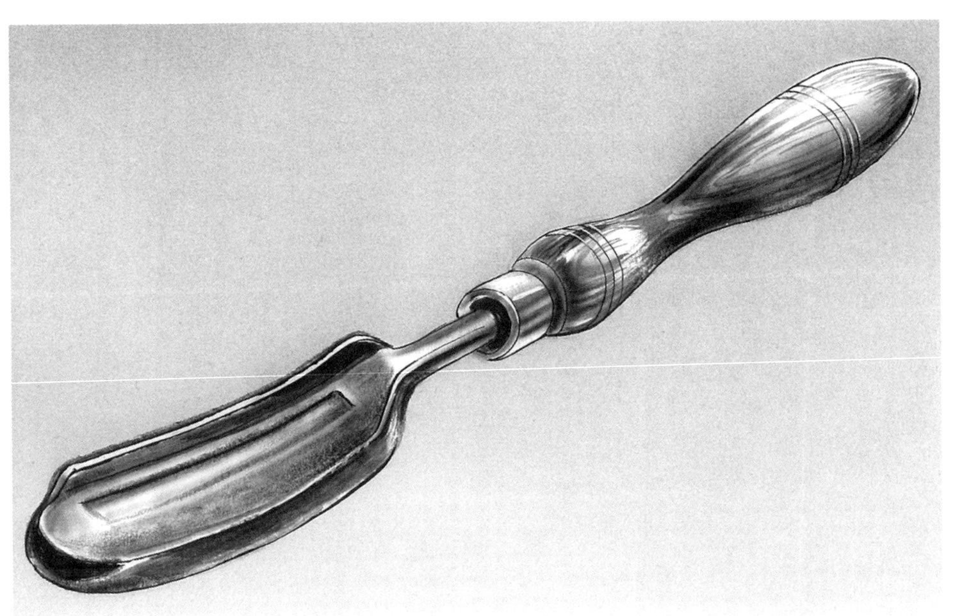

This item is a very solid piece of work, a foot long, with half its length taken up by a sturdy wooden handle and the other half a heavy steel section. The metal is slightly curved, with the outside face polished smooth, while the inside is still rough. One edge has a small lip which is also polished on the outside face. It has clearly been much used, but by whom and for what?

*answer on page 81*

This circular, plain wooden rod is fifteen inches long, and tapers smoothly from a six-inch diameter at the broad end to about two and half inches in diameter, and then tapers slightly more sharply to its point. The rod is heavy and seems quite old, so it is difficult to be sure whether the change in the angle of the taper is part of the original design or merely the result of wear and tear. A simple item — but is there a simple answer?

*answer on page 81*

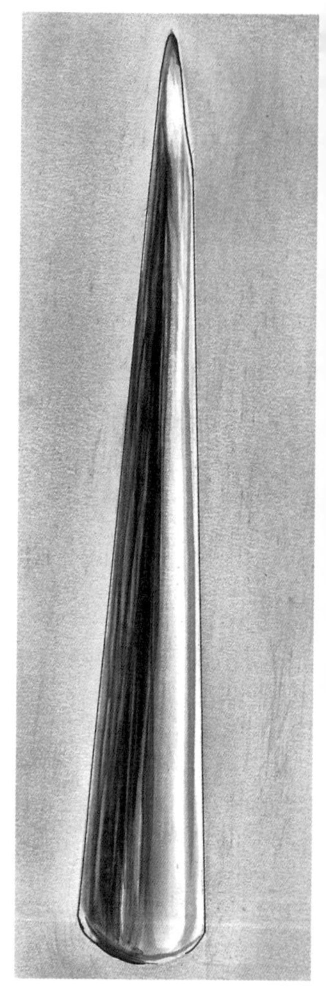

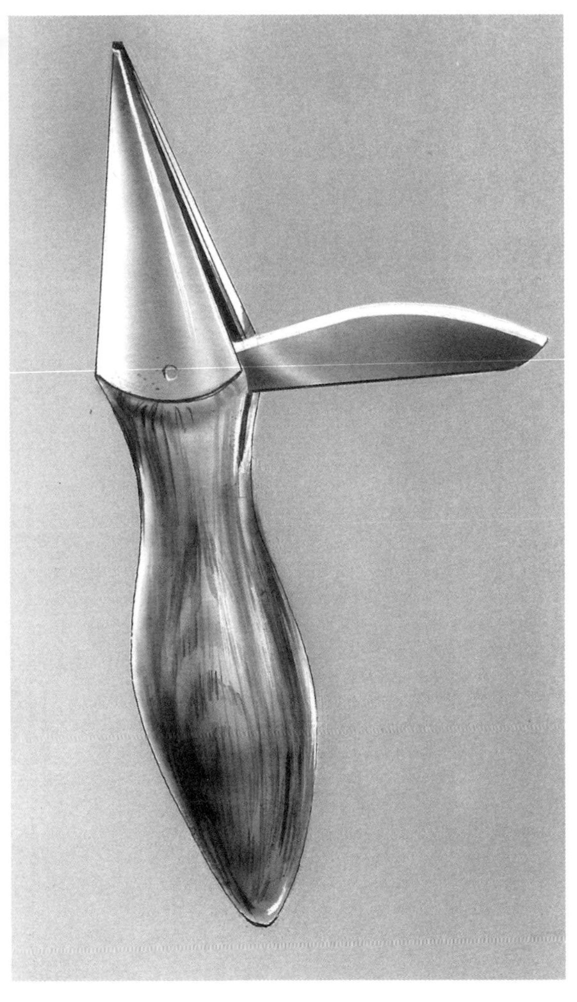

This gadget is obviously a very specialised knife. The sturdy wooden handle fits comfortably into the palm of the hand, and is attached to a tapering brass nose. The blade folds into the nose, rather like a penknife blade, and can be held in any position from totally shut to perpendicular with pressure from the thumb. There is no other method of fixing it in position. What was it for and who used it?

*answer on page 81*

This gadget is about three inches long and consists of an enclosed drum with a spool inside and a slit in the top. On the stem above are two metal rollers, and above them a highly polished dish with a hollow tube. What is it and what was it used for?

*answer on page 82*

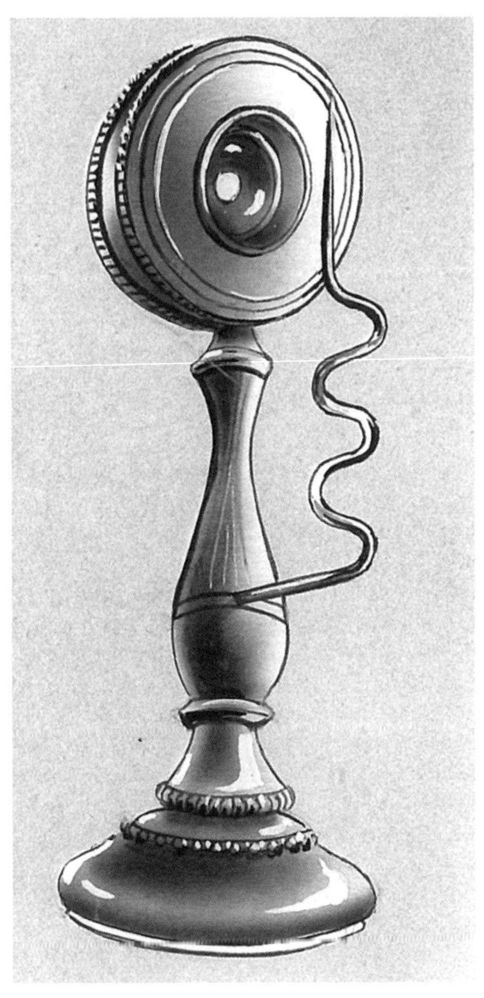

This object is as elegant as it is baffling. Standing just three inches tall, it is beautifully turned in dark wood. At the top of the stem is a circular piece of wood, the front of which has a dimpled recess, at the back of which is a small hole backed by a lens. At the back of the stem is a wire with several corrugations ending in a sharp point just above the level of the eyehole. What on earth was it used for?

*answer on page 82*

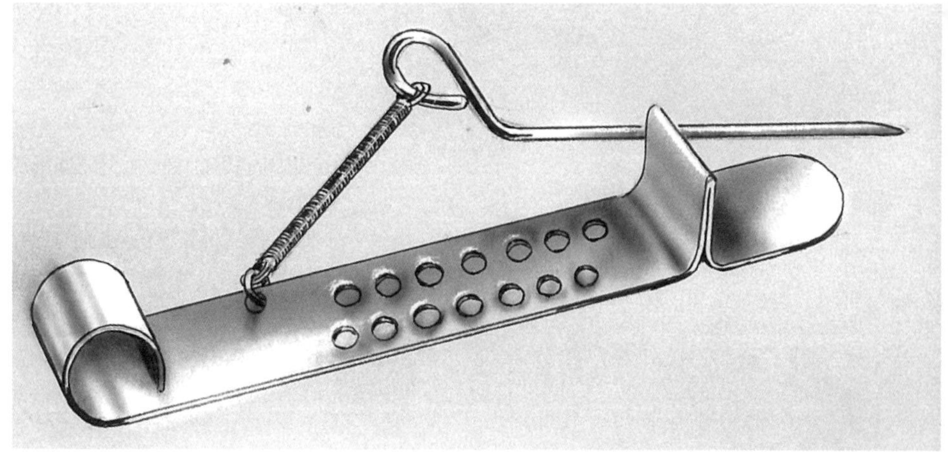

Made of shiny metal and a little over three inches long, this intriguing gizmo has a scrolled end and two rows of holes in the base plate. A long metal pin is attached to the side with a spring which allows the pin to be inserted into any of the holes. A sturdy device indeed — but for what purpose?

*answer on page 82*

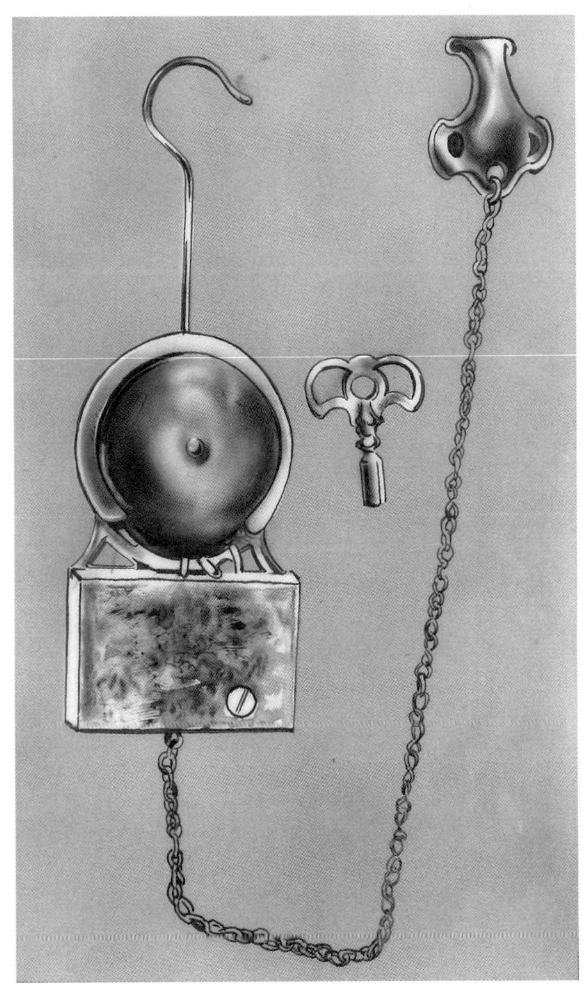

This is a complicated affair, consisting of a bell suspended from a small hook. Beneath the bell is a closed metal box with a winding key. Below that dangles a chain with a curved metal weight. An intriguing device, but what on earth was it for?

*answer on page 83*

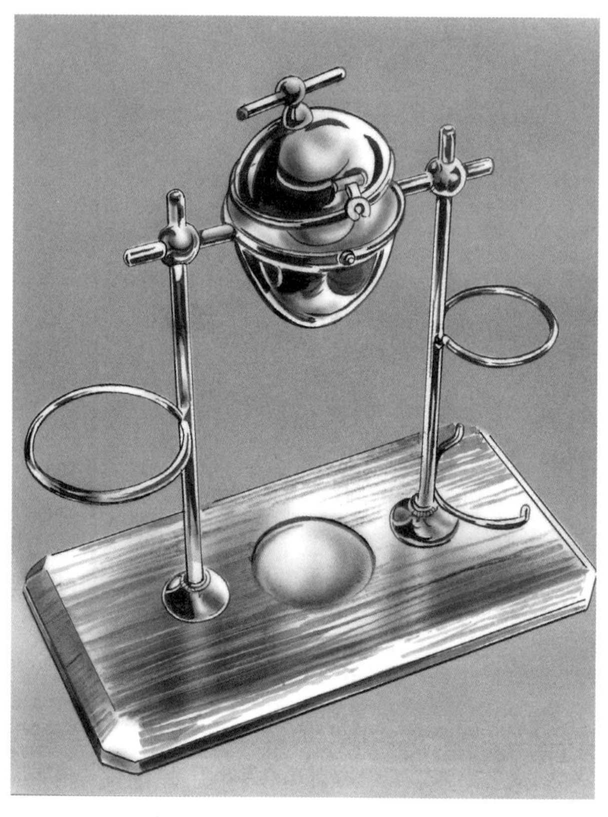

This handsome device was spotted in the bar of a hotel in the Forest of Bowland. Mounted on a polished wooden stand, the main part is a silver or chrome chamber with a hinged lid. Set in the lid is a threaded handle, like a corkscrew, but instead of a point it is attached to a wooden plunger inside the chamber. The bottom of the chamber is punctured by drain holes. On the two outside supports are metal rings which may have held glasses or supported bottles. Clearly it is a press of some description — but what did it press, and why so elaborate?

*answer on page 83*

This object is as tiny as it is intriguing. It is a flat metal disk about an inch and three quarters in diameter. One side is flat but on the other is a knurled button and when this is turned, a dozen quarter-inch-long blunt rods appear through slots in the rim. On the front is an Italian patent, but the article turned up among sewing materials at a home in Yorkshire. It is beautifully made and quite delicate. But what on earth is it?

*answer on page 83*

This device has a brutal simplicity, but it possesses an intriguing twist in the tail. It is ten inches long with a solid wooden handle. The square shaft tapers to a point with a bend near the end. The unexpected refinement, however, is a free-running blade which can slide up and down the shaft. It is pointed with sharpened edges and two runnels behind the blade. But what was it used for?

*answer on page 83*

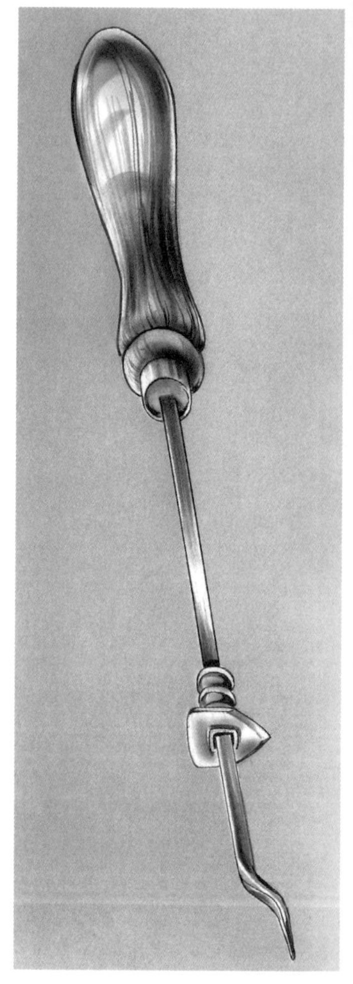

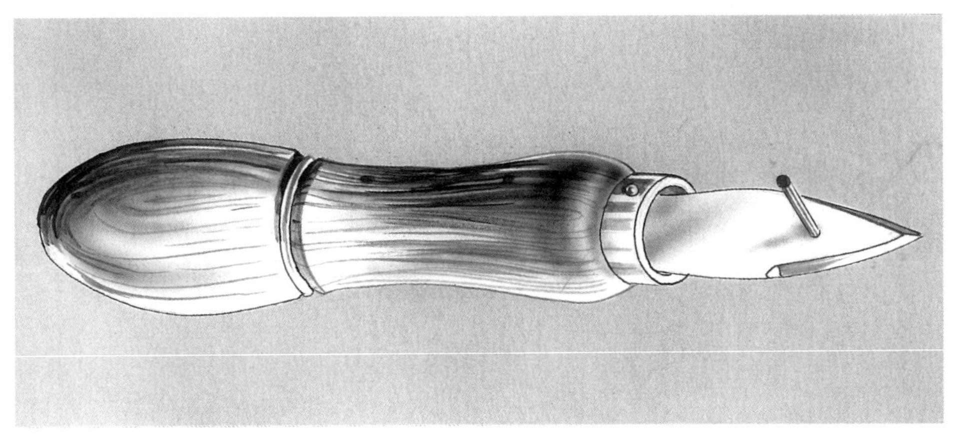

At first glance, this intriguing object is simple but comes with a baffling twist. It is clearly some kind of knife, a little under seven inches long with a short, pointed blade, bevelled on one face. The twist comes when the blade is turned over to show a round metal peg protruding at right angles from the flat side. What was it?

*answer on page 84*

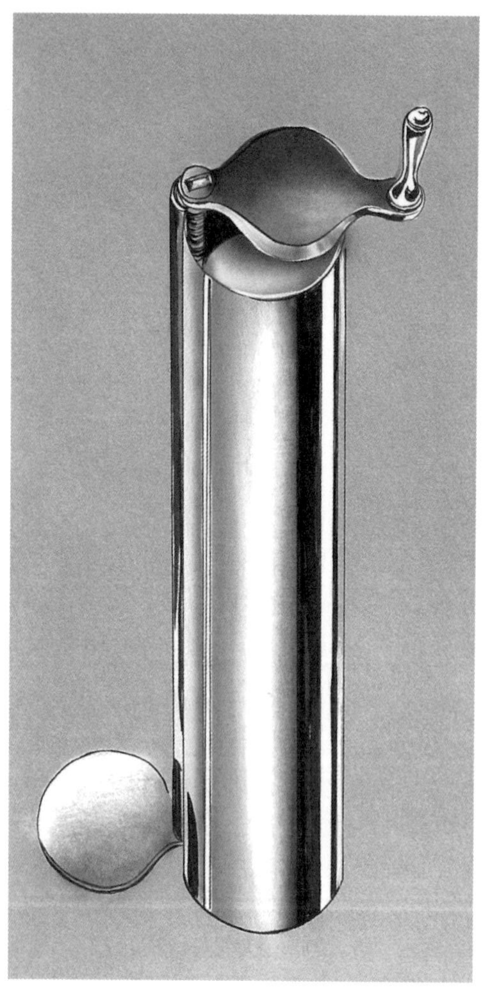

Here's a bewildering gadget which seems to be short of nothing but an apparent purpose. It is a brass cylinder, marked 'The Clifton', and is three inches long by about three-quarters of an inch in diameter. At one end is a pivoting cover. At the other end of the cylinder is a handle which turns a spindle and plunger inside the cylinder. The handle also acts as a cover for the end of the barrel, and is sharpened on one side so that anything being forced up the barrel by the plunger would be sliced on each turn of the handle. But what would it have sliced?

*answer on page 84*

This object reveals at least part of its mystery immediately. It is a compass of sorts, but clearly one designed to keep its user on the straight and narrow since it deviates only 5° either side of north. Perhaps it would suit a particularly obsessive polar explorer? Or if not, who?

*answer on page 84*

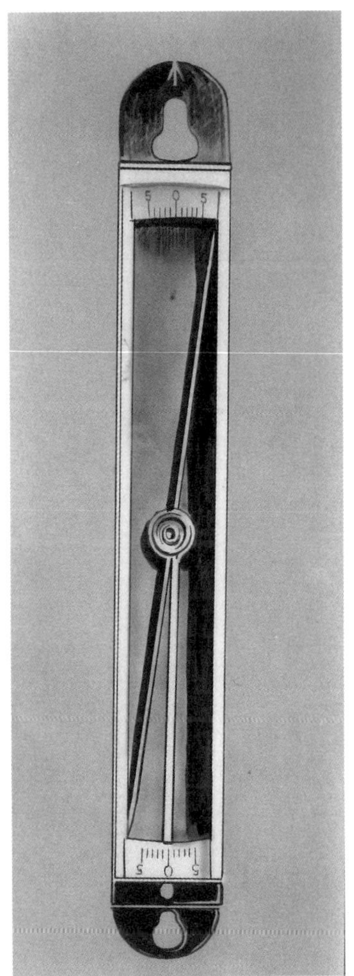

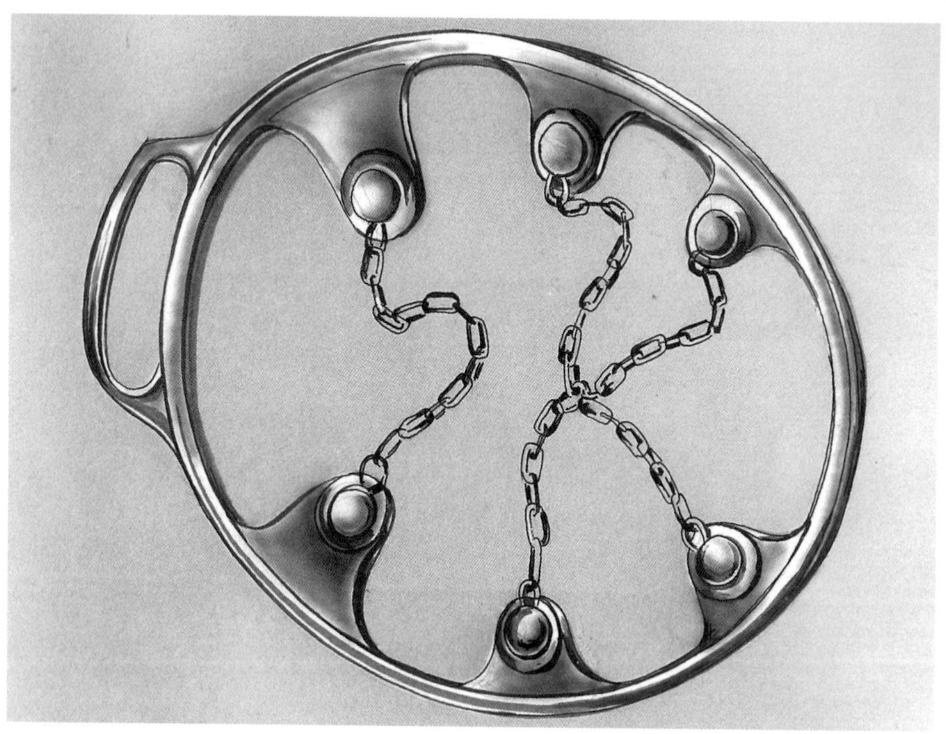

This drawing features one of a pair. It is a circle of stout rubber, criss-crossed by thin but sturdy chains. One chain runs across the ring in a single strand, but the two others cross in the centre. What on earth was this and its companion used for?

*answer on page 85*

This item is made of brass, and measures about five inches in diameter and an inch and half tall. A small segment lifts open to reveal three toothed cardboard wheels, which are turned by a knurled wheel on the top. The wheels are very worn, and at one time may have been bigger. The roughened top looks as if it is inlaid with red.

*answer on page 85*

This object is a pair of ... well, what? They open like pliers, but the two curved blades do not touch even when closed. If the clasp at the opposite end is fastened, the two blades still remain about a tenth of an inch apart. When the clasp is released, the leaf spring opens them to a gap of about an inch and a quarter. On one arm is a fixed rod which seems designed to ensure the handles can be squeezed firmly together, yet the blades are blunt and show no signs of ever having been sharpened. What on earth were they for?

*answer on page 85*

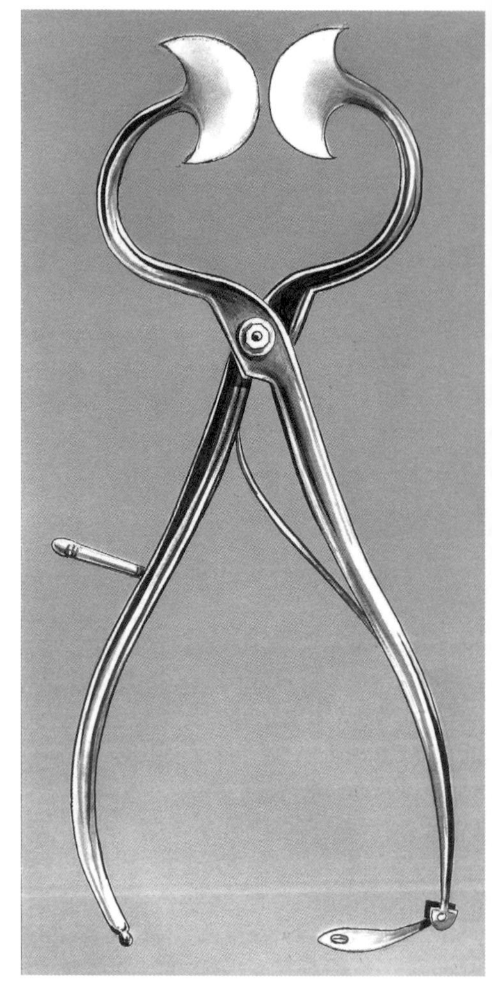

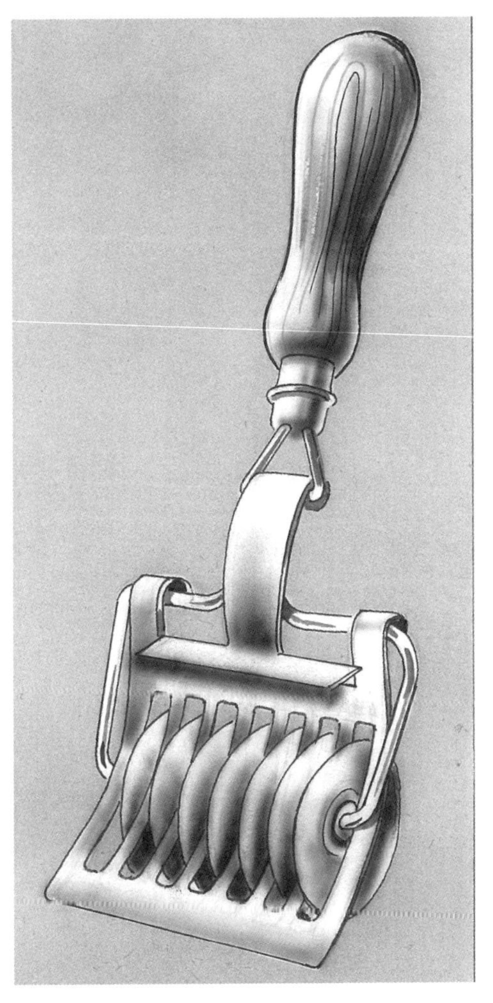

This intriguing object has a handle attached to a metal frame and grid, in front of which is a set of seven sharp wheels which may have been blades and which fit through the slots in the frame. It has all the hallmarks of being a cunning household gadget that may have once been common in the kitchen but has now been replaced by more modern gizmos. So what was it and what was it used for?

*answer on page 85*

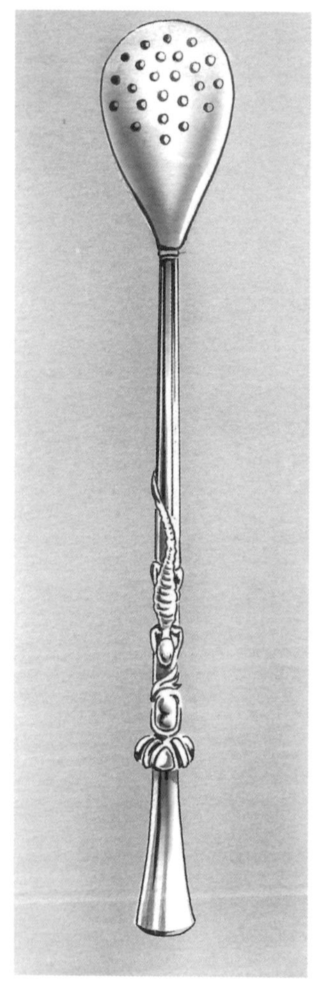

Today's use for this might very well be to decorate a cosy fireplace, or perhaps to hang on a cottage beam. But no doubt it had an earlier, more practical, use. It is made of silver and about eight inches long. At one end of the hollow tube is what appears to be a mouthpiece, while the other end is bulbous and perforated. What on earth was this delicate instrument used for?

*answer on page 86*

This item has a homely feel to it. An ivory-handled knife, it is six inches long with a distinctive hooked blade. The blade is sharp all the way up the unhooked side, but sharp only on the final half inch of the hooked side. The recessed part is blunt. The shape suggests it had a very special use — but what was it?

*answer on page 86*

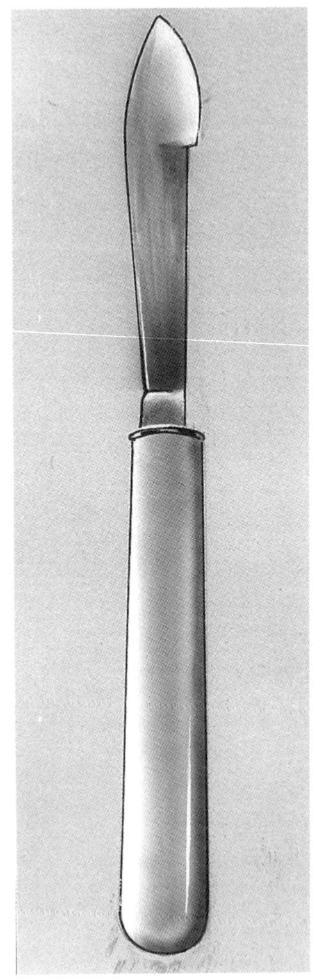

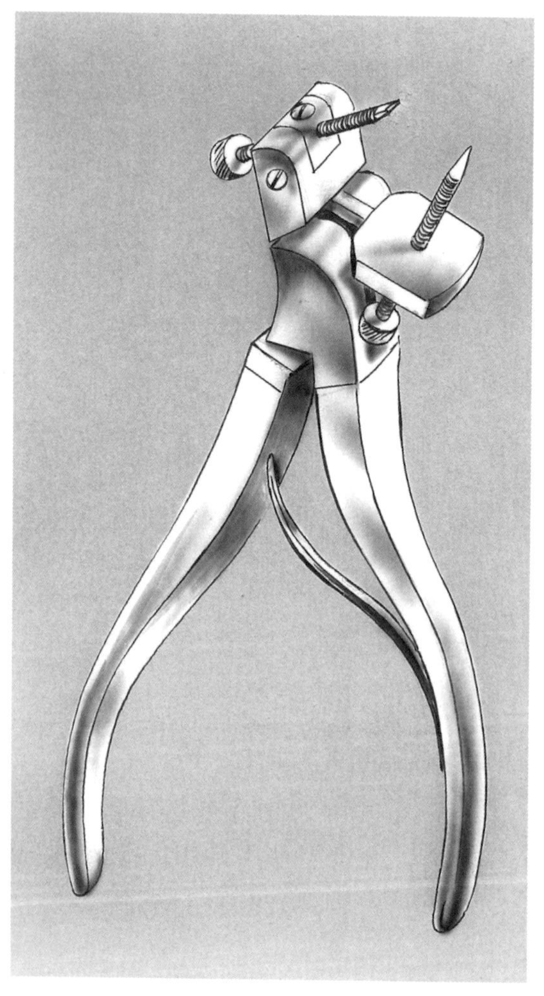

This well-made device is about six inches long with two threaded spikes in the jaws. They can be adjusted to either touch or leave a gap and one has a small nick in the end while the other is pointed. What is it and what was it used for?

*answer on page 86*

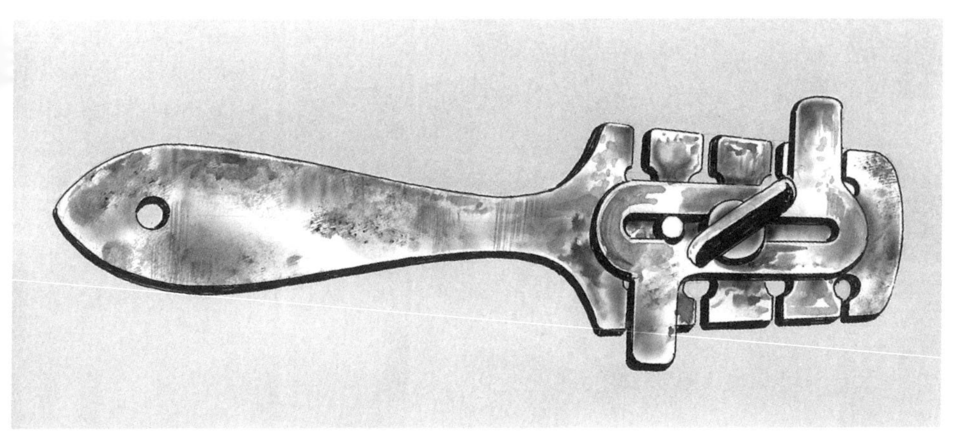

This object is metal, almost flat and a little over five inches long. The head tapers slightly and has a series of five keyhole-shaped holes up each side, all open, with the slots getting thinner towards the top of the head. One side has a bracket with offset arms which can slide up or down, but which is held in line by a peg and a wing nut which can also lock the slider into position, with the arms blocking off some of the holes. But who used it, and for what?

*answer on page 86*

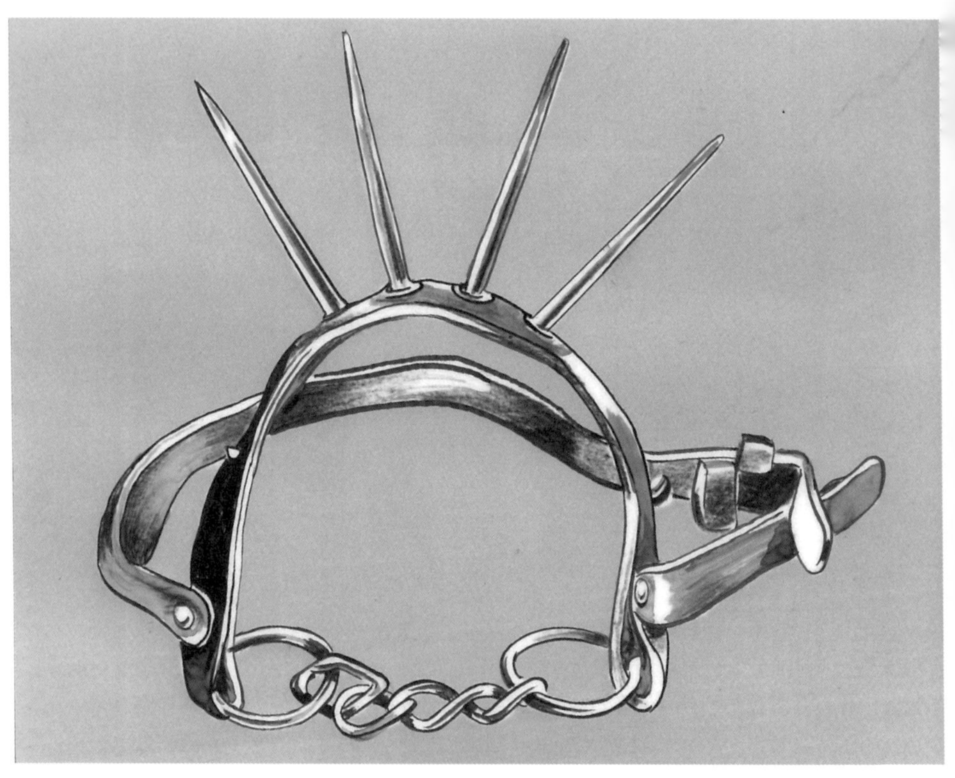

This gruesome device looks as though it belongs in some medieval dungeon or fastened around the neck of a spectral hound. It has a leather loop surmounted by a fan of four metal spikes with another strap at 90° to the first. It looks very painful — but for who?

*answer on page 87*

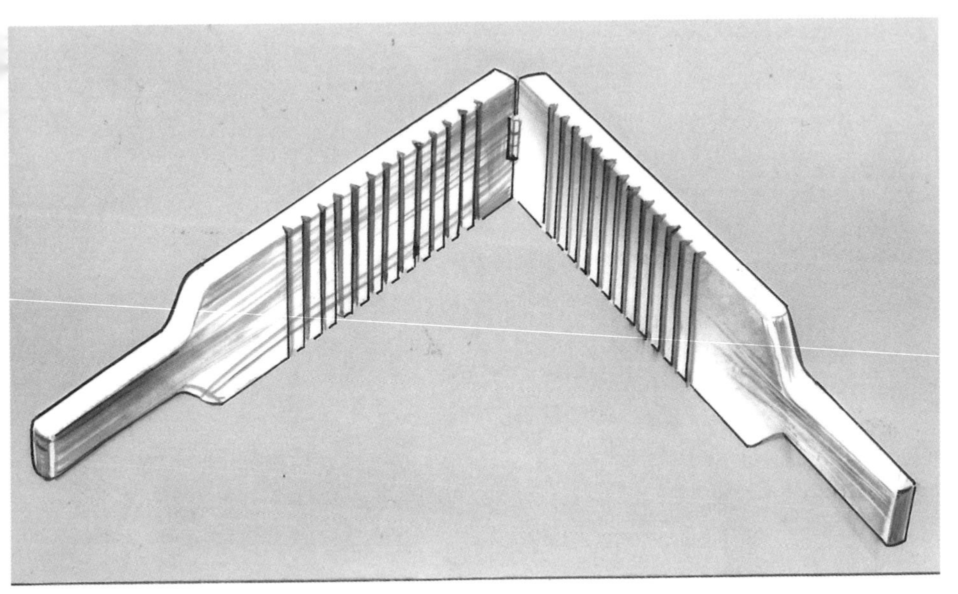

This hinged device came from a farm in the Yorkshire Dales. The two wooden arms are four and a half inches wide and nineteen inches long. Each has thirteen notches carved into the full width of the handles, so that when it is closed it creates a series of diamond-shaped holes. The notches are three-quarters of an inch apart and a quarter of an inch deep.

*answer on page 87*

This item looks like the garden variety but is far from common. It is spade length, with a standard spade handle and a metal crosspiece to enable a foot to drive it into the ground. However, instead of a blade it has a two-pronged fork and on the back is a curl of metal. But what was it for?

*answer on page 87*

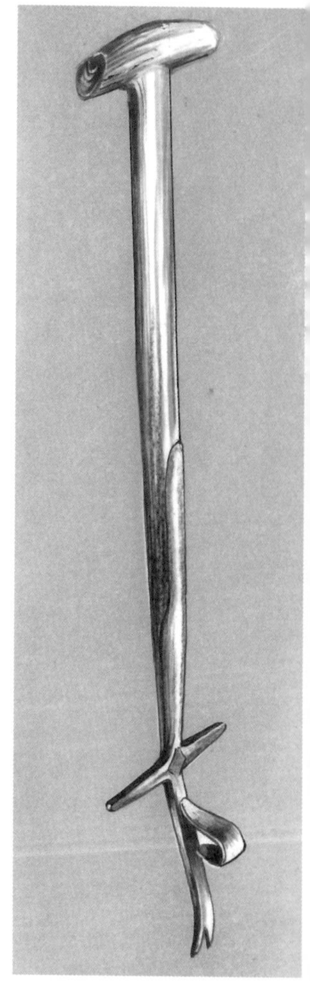

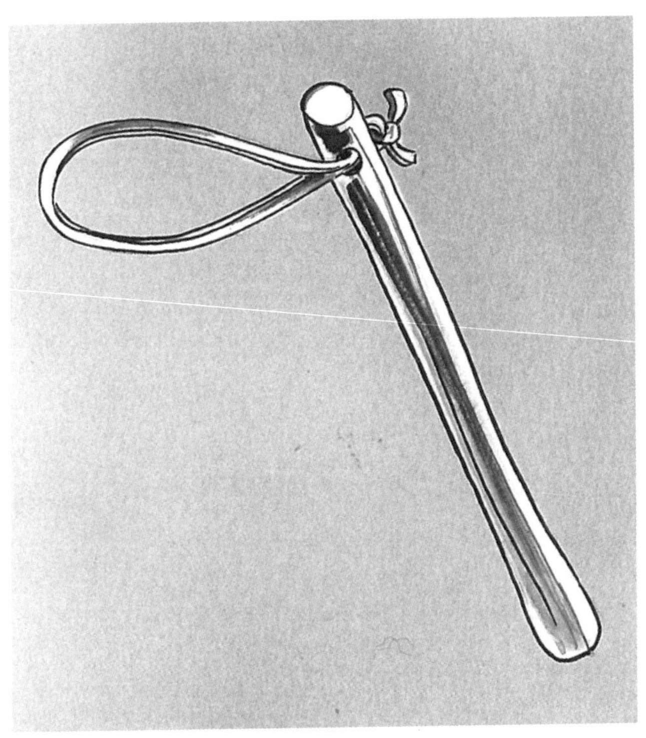

This short piece of wood, eighteen inches long and slightly thicker than a broom handle, has two holes drilled through one end and a short leather thong pushed through in a way that allows the loop to be tightened or loosened. At first it looks like a truncheon, but the wood is too light to be very effective. So what was it used for?

*answer on page 87*

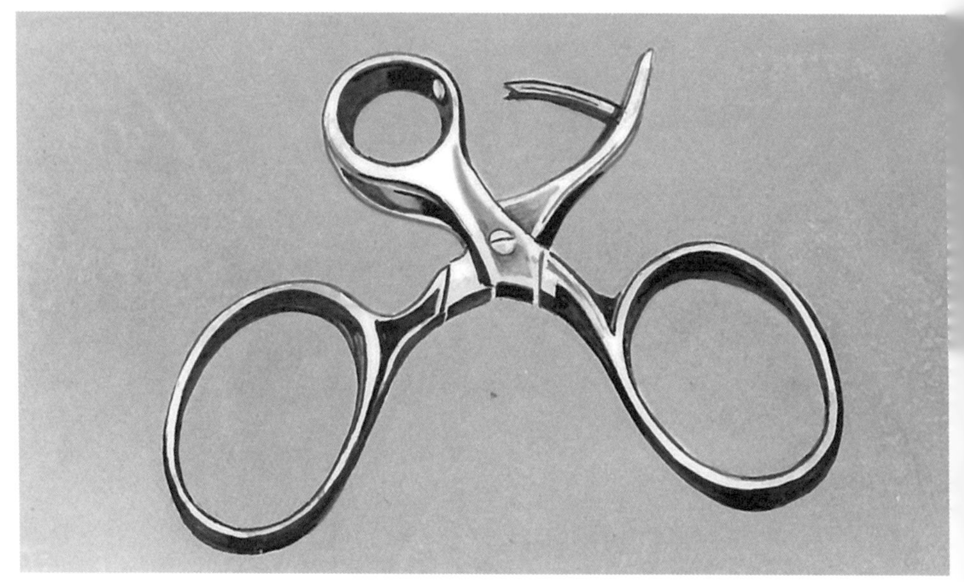

This intriguing item resembles a small pair of scissors but with a couple of crucial differences. They are two and a half inches long but, instead of blades, one arm has a small metal ring, slightly bigger than finger size, while the other sports a small spike which slots through a hole in the side of the ring when the arms are closed. The spike is obviously intended to pierce whatever was held in the ring. But what was it?

*answer on page 88*

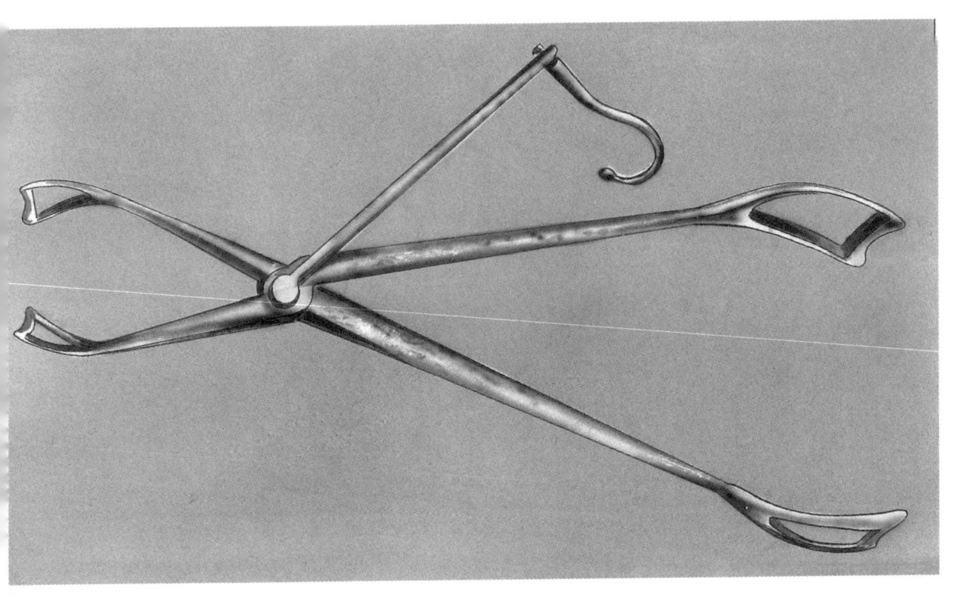

This gruesome-looking device is clearly the product of much thought. It is fifteen inches long and appears to be a set of reversible tongs. The shorter arms measure five inches and end in a pair of identical grips. The longer pair, which are ten inches long, have ends of similar design though one is smaller than the other. The other arm is about nine inches long and ends in a blunt hook which is hinged to bend through 90°. But what could it possibly have been used for?

*answer on page 88*

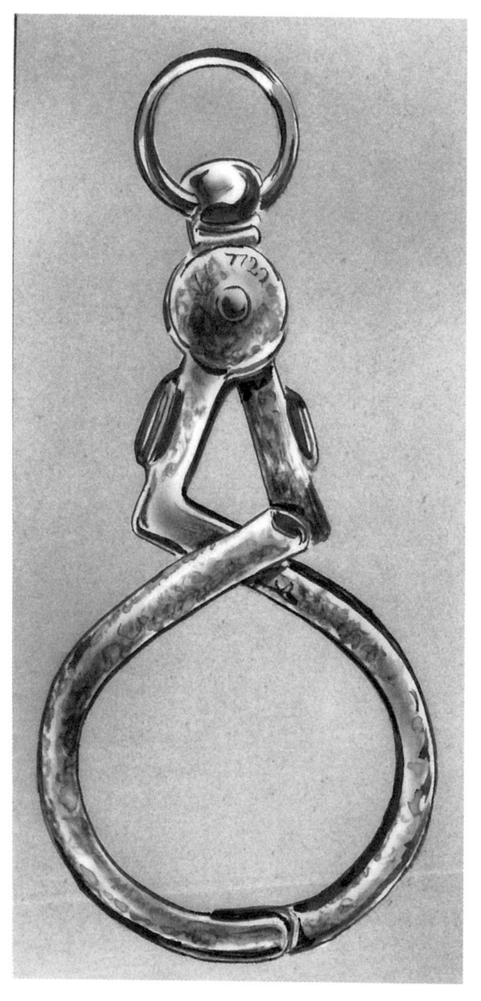


This spring-loaded metal clip, about three inches long, normally forms a closed loop, as illustrated here, but when the two upper arms are squeezed together they allow the two halves of the loop to open. The two parts of the loop slot together with overlapping sections, but there is no latch or lock to ensure it remains closed. At the other end is a smaller and less sturdy ring. What on earth was it and who used it?

*answer on page 88*

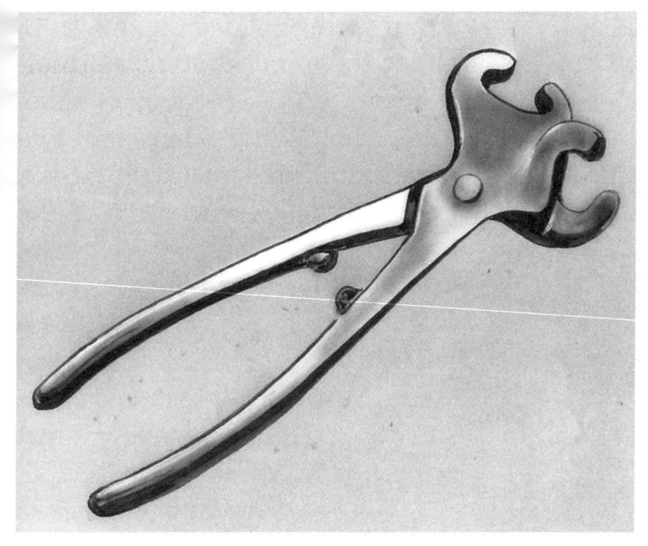

This pair — or is it two pairs? — of pincers seems to have belonged to someone who liked to work quickly. Perhaps the need for speed meant he did not have time to put down one pair to pick up another. Or perhaps he just had limited space in his toolbox. When the handles are opened, both sets of jaws open, though one is slightly wider than the other, opening to about one and a half inches across, while its neighbour is slightly smaller. Did they just belong to a man in a hurry — or was there a special purpose for them?

*answer on page 88*

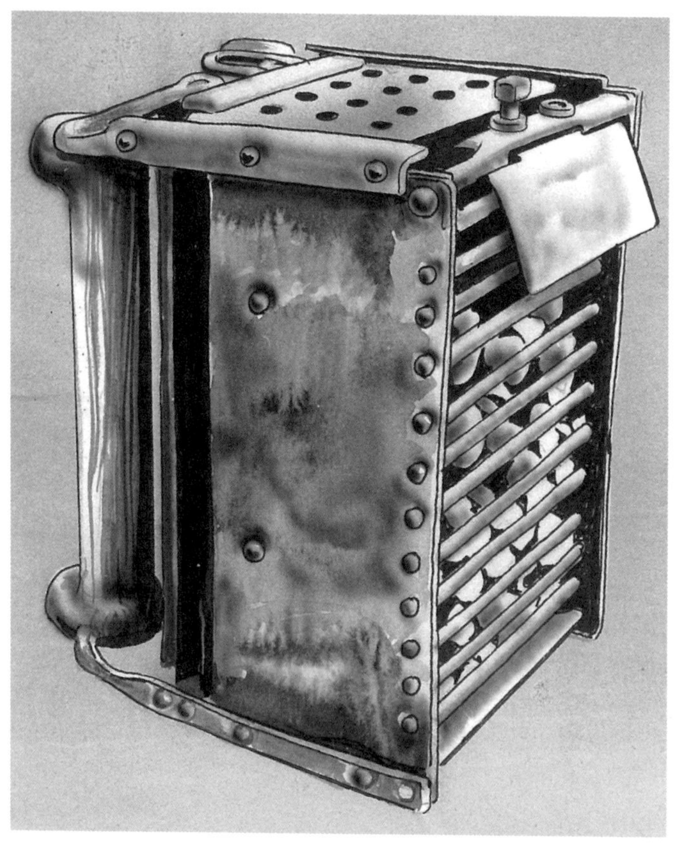

This device is a chunky piece of work, made from solid iron. It is a metal box about seven inches high with a barred front. Above the slats is a downward-pointing metal strip. On the back of the box are a pair of hefty wooden handles. The base of the box seems to contain traces of what may have been charcoal. But what on earth was it for?

*answer on page 89*

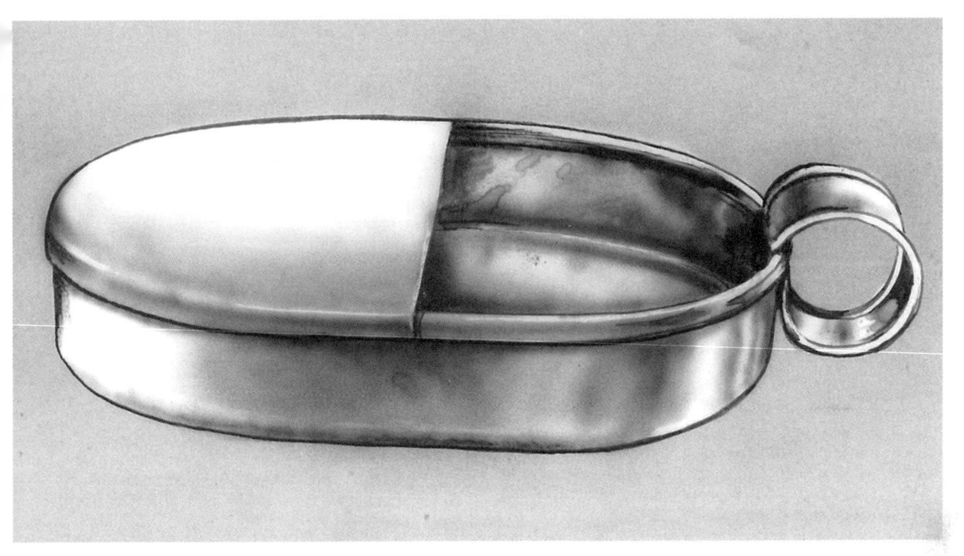

At first glance this object may look like a half-opened sardine tin, but it is a little more elaborate than that. For a start, it is made of brass and has clearly been fashioned with some care. The body is five inches long and three and a quarter inches wide. The half nearer the handle is open, while that further away is covered, and the whole is held together by a strip of copper.

*answer on page 89*

This elegant object once stood on a chest of drawers. Made of mahogany, the central spike rises from the centre of the polished base and ends in a cross. What on earth is it?

*answer on page 89*

This item looks as though it may have graced a Victorian dresser or mantelpiece. It is a little over seven inches tall and more than seventeen inches around, made of glass and stands on three glass feet. It has a tight-fitting glass stopper in the top, but was clearly not meant to be airtight as in the base there is a hole large enough to fit a hand through. What could it have been used for?

*answer on page 90*

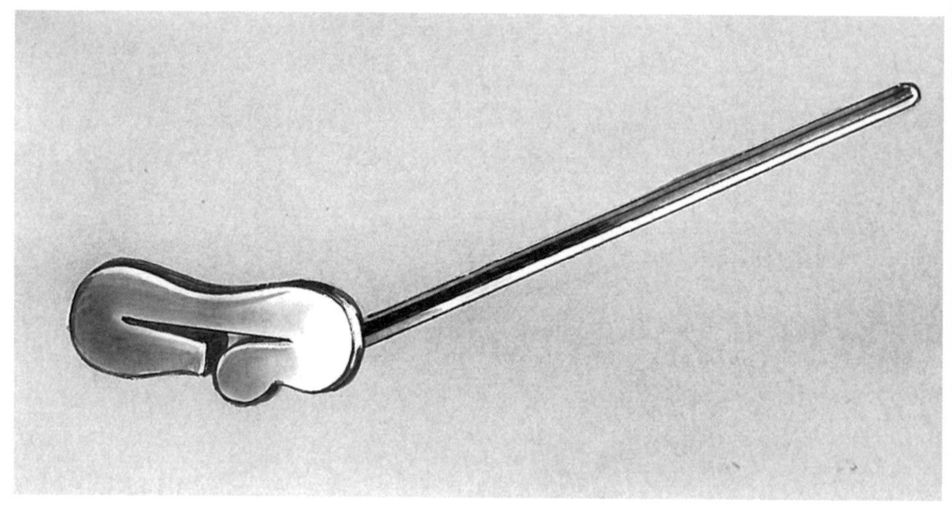

This device is made of a white metal and has a three-inch-long stem which ends in a flattened shoe. It was found in a box together with a number of crochet hooks. But what could it have been used for?

*answer on page 90*

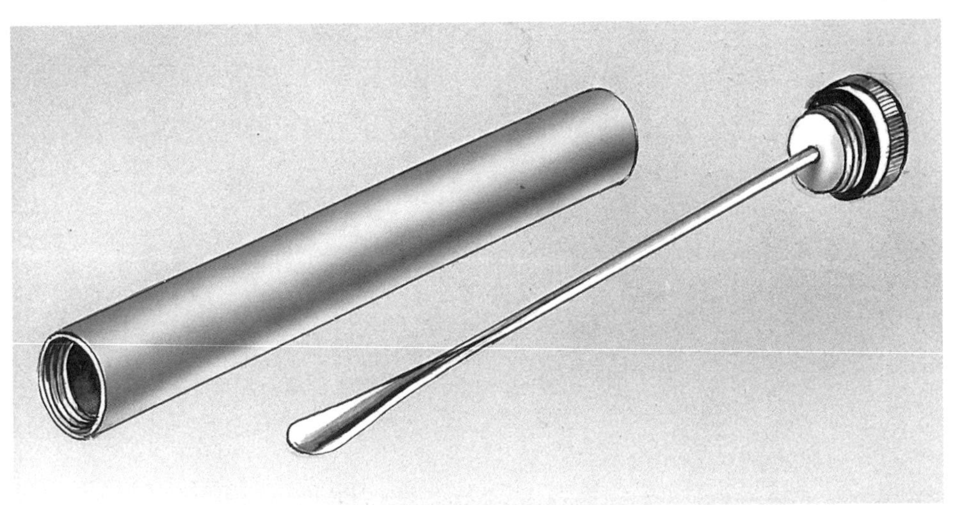

This object is bafflingly simple. It consists of a brass cylinder, approximately three and a half inches long. The top screws off to reveal a rubber seal. Attached to the inside of the top is a three-inch steel rod with a curved and grooved end. What on earth was it for?

*answer on page 90*

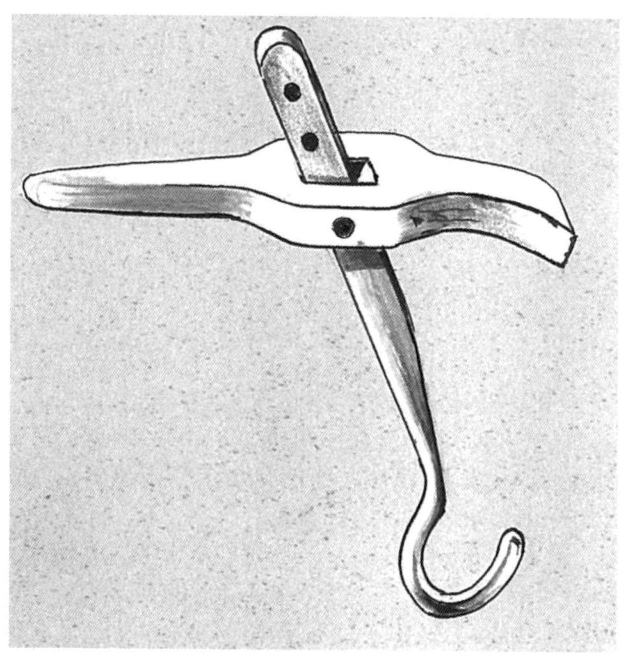

This item has a distinctly rustic air, and looks as though it may have been languishing in a barn or outhouse for many years. It consists of a now somewhat rusty iron hook, approximately fourteen inches long, which fits through a pivoting wooden spar of similar length. The spar, which has suffered the attention of woodworm, has a blunt spike at one end and a squared-off blunt adze shape at the other. It is a simple-enough looking tool, but what on earth was it for?

*answer on page 90*

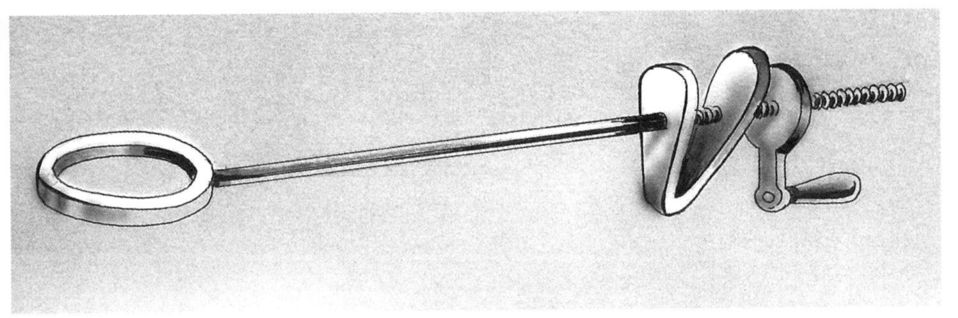

This is a study piece of craftsmanship. It consists of an iron ring six inches in diameter with a three-foot-long iron rod. The end away from the rod is threaded with a handle that can be turned to wind it along the rod, pushing a V-shaped bit of metal in front of it. What was this strange contraption used for?

*answer on page 91*

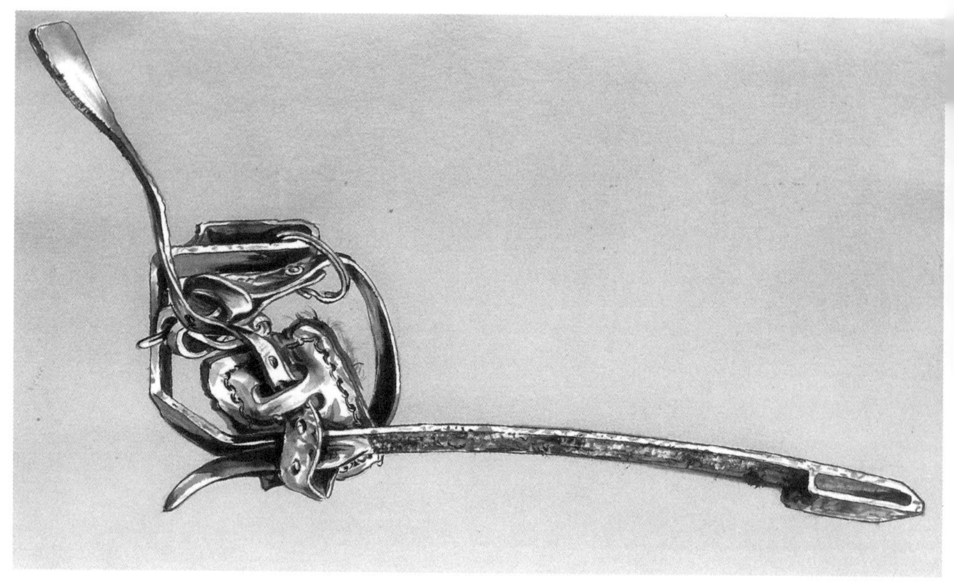

This rusting relic is one of a pair, and is made of heavy iron bent into an ‘L’ shape eighteen inches long with a bottom bar four and half inches across. Just above the bend is a padded leather strap which runs through a bracket and a ring. On the outside of the bend is a short metal spike. But what was this and its companion used for?

*answer on page 91*

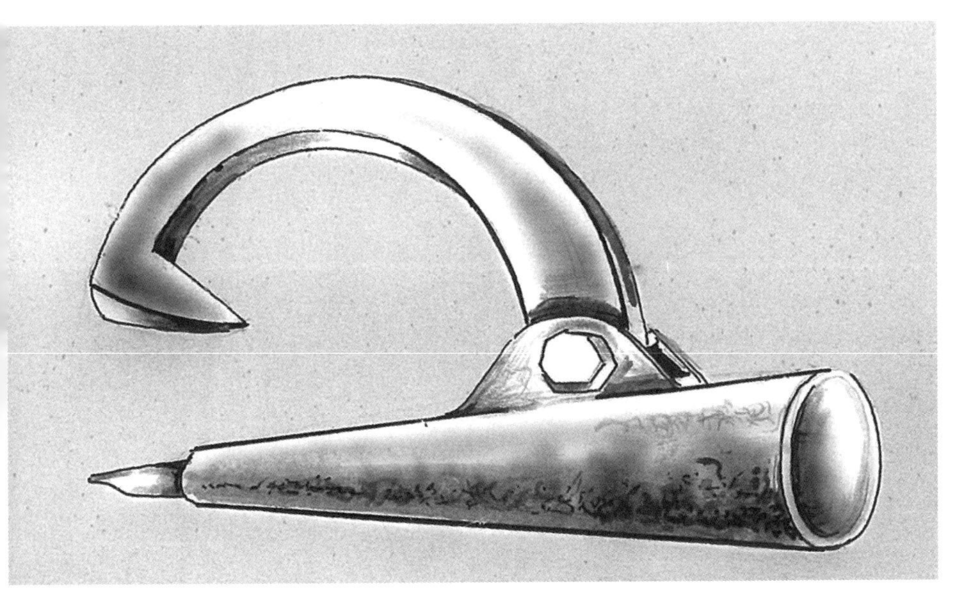

This solid piece of metalwork, rusted and pitted from what has all the hallmarks of long and heavy use, consists of a nine-inch tapered spike, the broad end of which is hollow and looks as if it once held a wooden shaft. To the side is a pivoted hook, now fairly stiff with rust but which may once have moved much more freely. But what could it have been used for?

*answer on page 92*

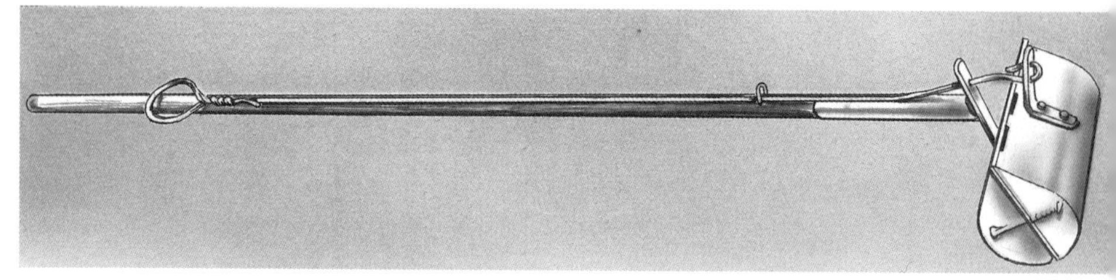

This item looks as though it may have been designed for dealing with those things no one would want to touch with the proverbial barge pole. It consists of an almost cylindrical metal hopper mounted on a six-foot-long handle. The hopper is spring loaded, and can be opened and closed remotely by a wire running up the handle. What on earth was it that the operator wanted to keep his or her distance from?

*answer on page 92*

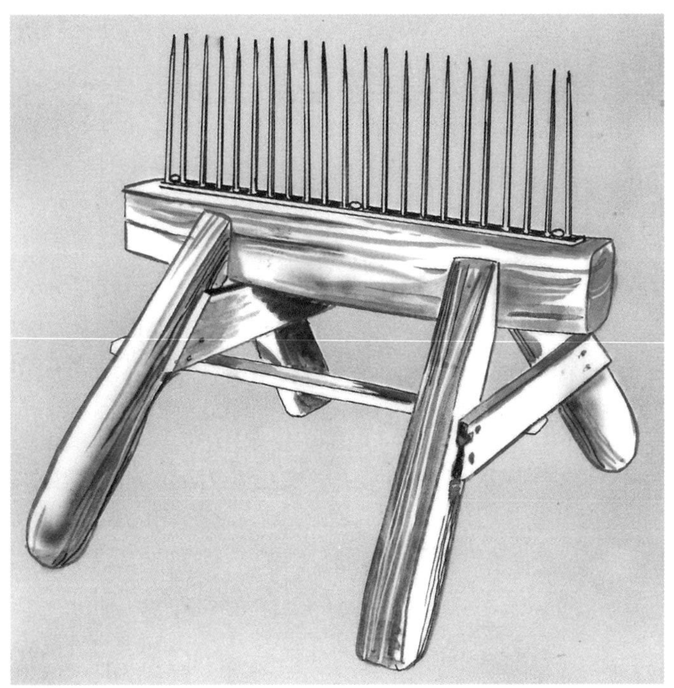

This implement has a workman-like rustic feel to it — and the appearance of an instrument that might have been quite at home in a medieval torture chamber. It is a solid wooden trestle, a little over two feet high, surmounted by a row of slightly blunt metal spikes, each fifteen inches long. It clearly means business — but what sort of business exactly?

*answer on page 92*

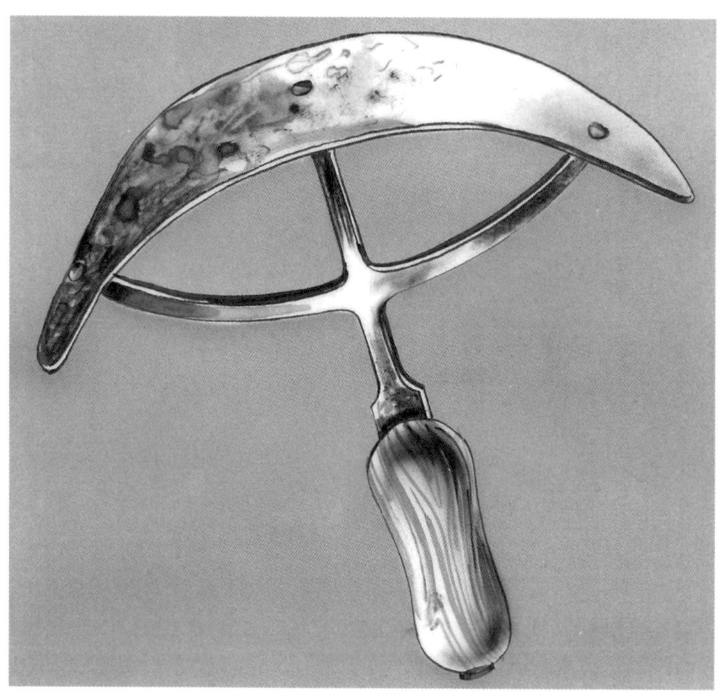

This object has been around for a long time. It is well made and definitely not a 'one-off'. The sturdy wooden handle is less than a foot long and ends in a curved base just over nine inches long and two inches wide. The shape suggests it was used for pressing or rolling something, and the bracing struts indicate a fair bit of pressure may have been needed. But on what?

*answer on page 92*

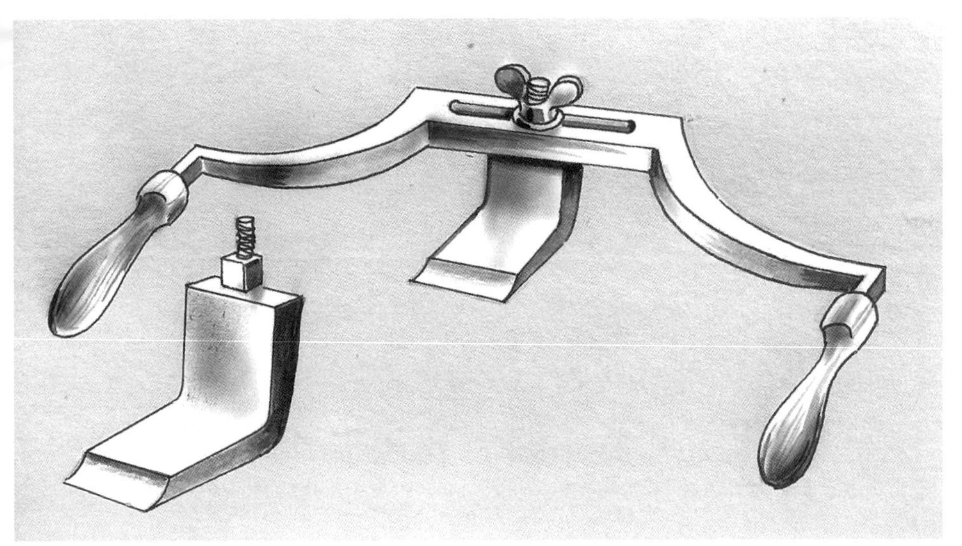

This item is clearly a variation on the traditional draw knife, used by woodworkers through the centuries. This particular model, however, has an interesting variation in that it has an interchangeable angled blade, which suggests it was used for a more specific purpose than merely generally shaping wood. But what purpose?

*answer on page 93*

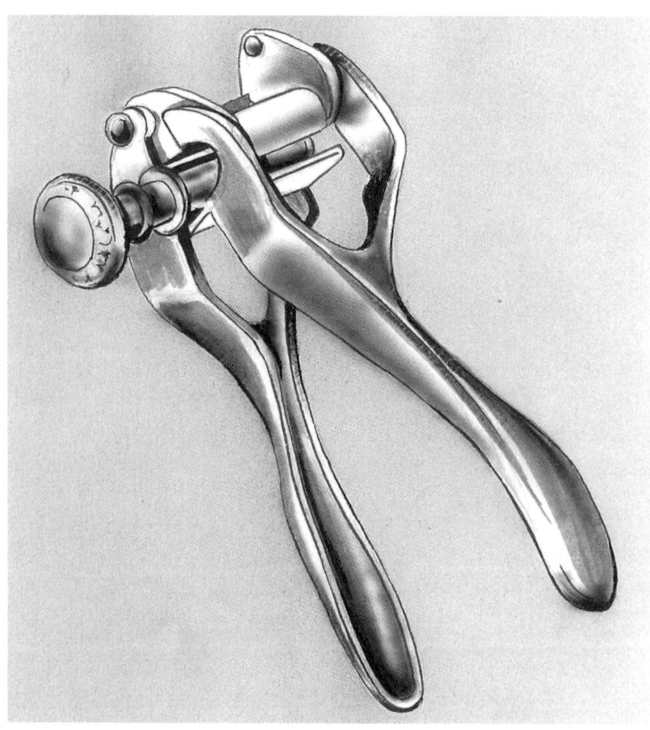

This item is a hefty piece of brasswork that sits purposefully in the hand. Its arms open to 180° but close to form a three-quarter-inch diameter tube a little over two inches long. A steel plunger with a worn brass head fits easily through the tube. But what on earth could it have been used for?

*answer on page 93*

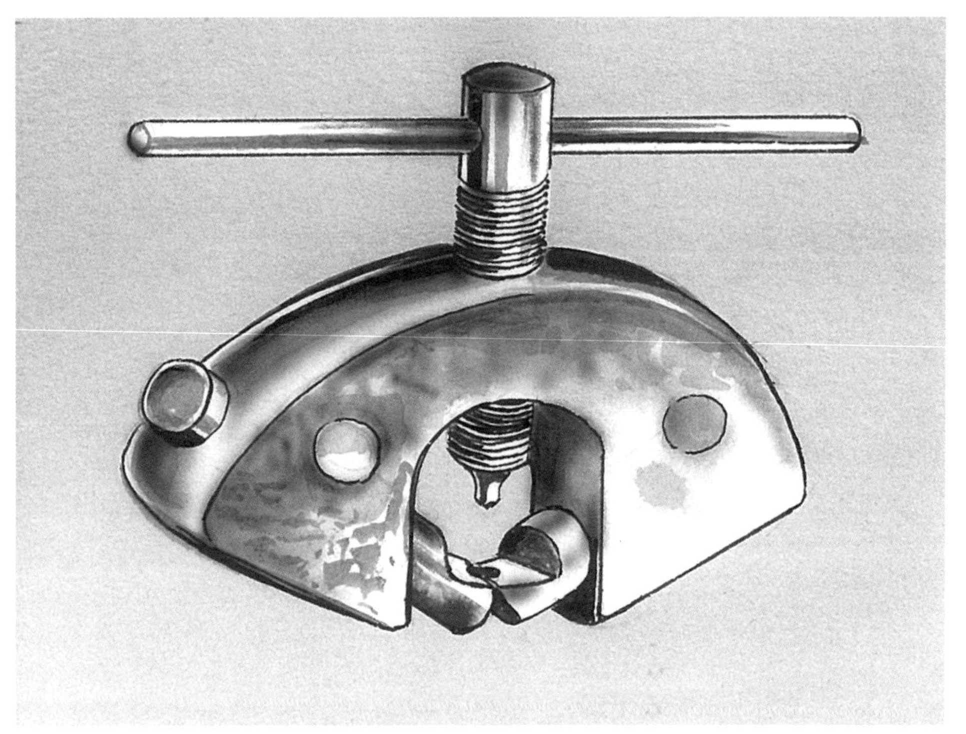

This item is a solidly made steel tool that fits easily into the palm of the hand. At the top of the horseshoe-shaped slot is a threaded pin which can be wound up and down, while at the bottom are two angled pins which can slide easily in and out to meet in the middle. A simple enough device, but what is it for?

*answer on page 93*

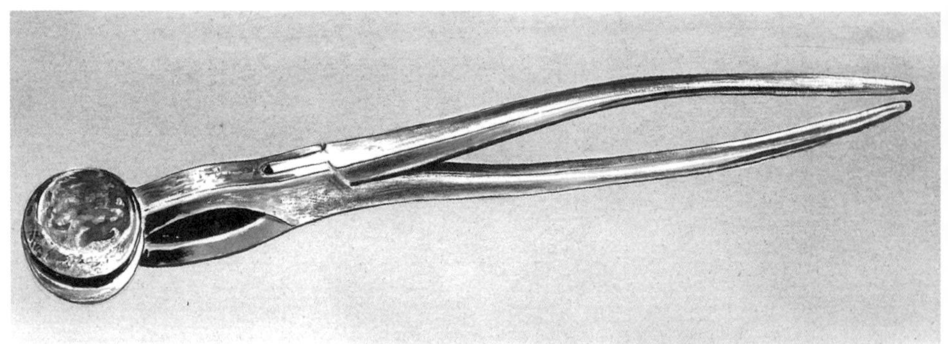

This item is a familiar object with an unusual twist. It is clearly a pair of pincers or tongs, but one that seems to have a specialised purpose. In place of the jaws is a pair of smooth flat discs slightly larger than a two-pence piece, totally flat and leaving a slight gap even when the handles are closed. Other than perhaps making very small pancakes, what on earth were they used for?

*answer on page 93*

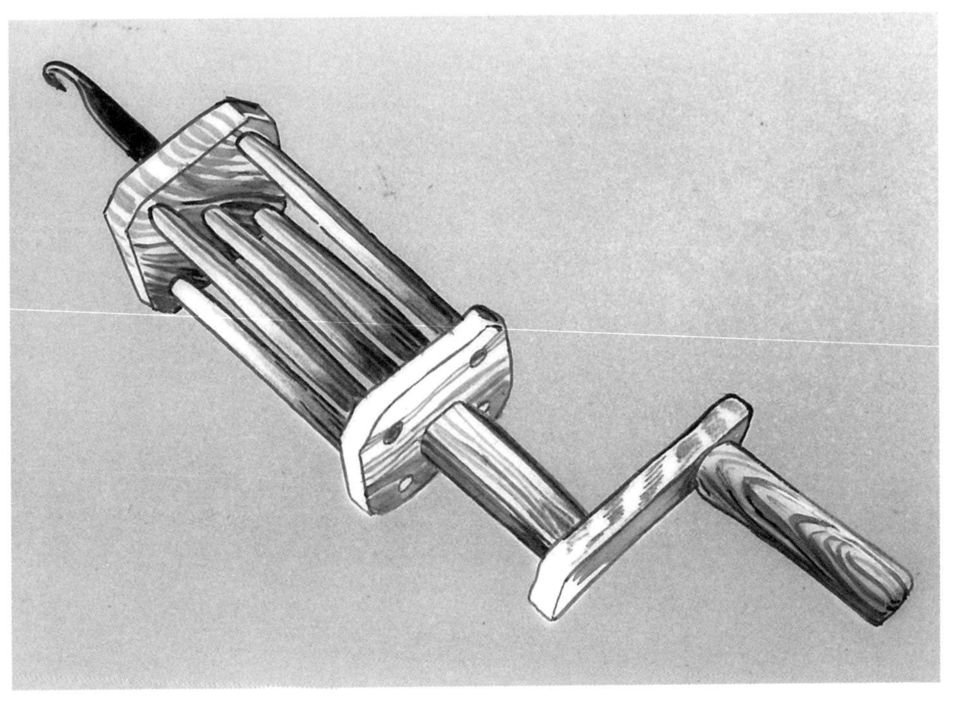

Essentially a spindle partly enclosed in a wooden cage, this object has a handle at one end and a metal hook at the other. A simple enough design, but what was it used for and by whom?

*answer on page 94*

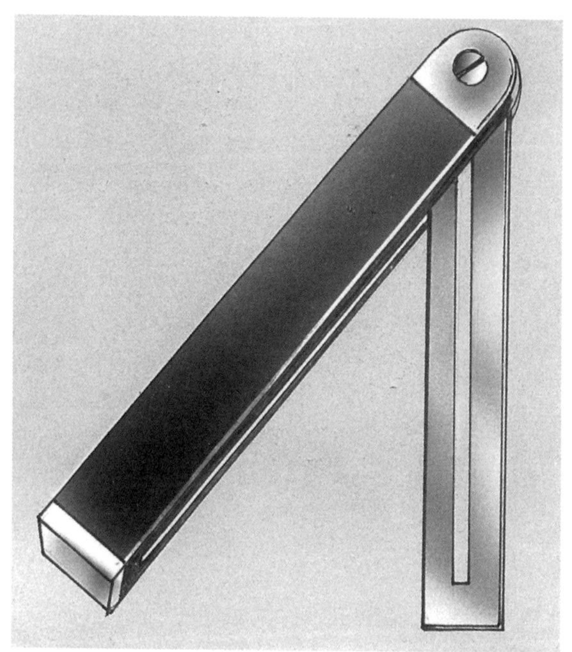

At first glance this item may look like a penknife, but it would need a large pocket to contain it. The handle, made of ebony with brass ends, is a foot long and a little over an inch wide, and slightly less than an inch thick. The 'blade' is not sharpened but is square cut with a slot down the centre. The screw which fastens it to the handle can be tightened and loosened to move the metal arm or to lock it into any position. But what could it have been used for?

*answer on page 94*

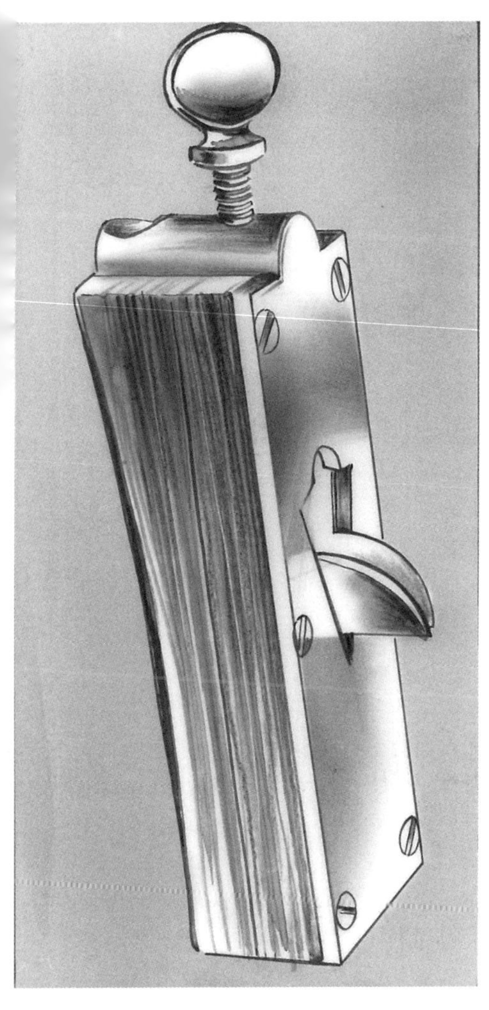

This was obviously a workman's tool. It is a small block of wood a little over four inches long by an inch and a half or so wide and deep, and fits neatly into the palm of the hand. The 'business end' is a brass plate, into which is cut a V-slot holding two angled blades. The distance between the blades can be altered by turning a screw at the back. An interesting tool, but what on earth was it for?

*answer on page 94*

This item is a precision piece, a thin metal tube, just three inches long with a metal loop at one end. Inside is a glass 'egg timer'. But the timer runs for exactly thirty seconds and is marked '½ min' on the side. So, other than timing extremely soft boiled eggs, what was it for and who used it?

*answer on page 94*

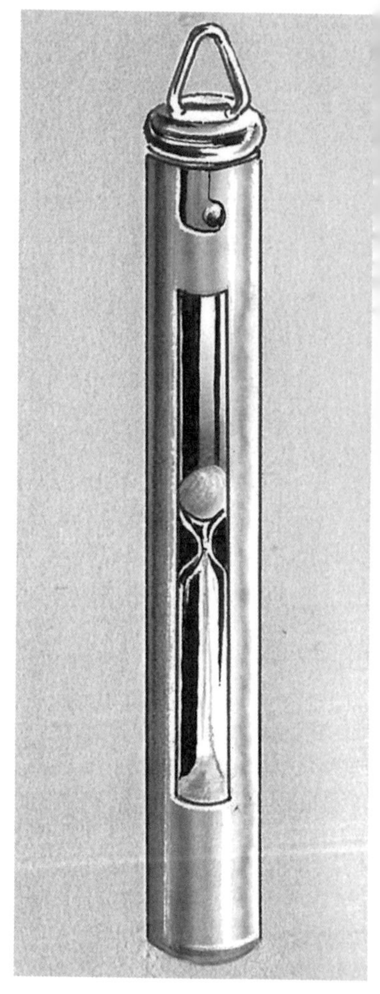

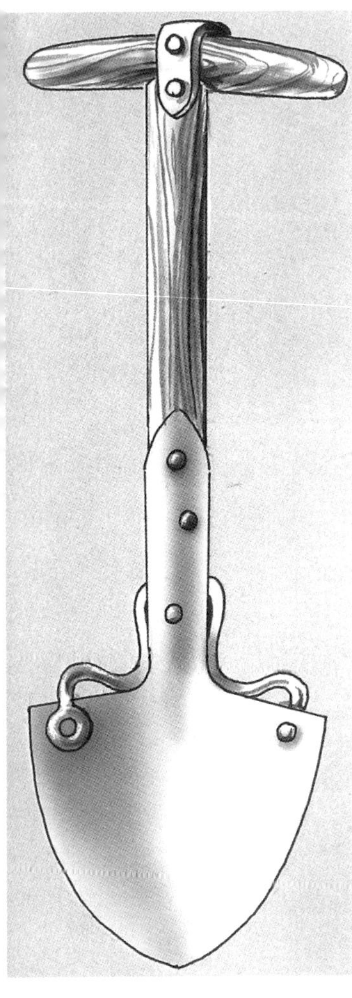

This is obviously a spade, but clearly it is designed for something a little more specialised than simply digging the vegetable patch on a Sunday morning. Its broad blade is pointed but the really unusual element is the pair of struts running from the shaft to the top of the blade, one attached to the front and the other to the back. Very distinctive but what on earth was it for?

*answer on page 95*

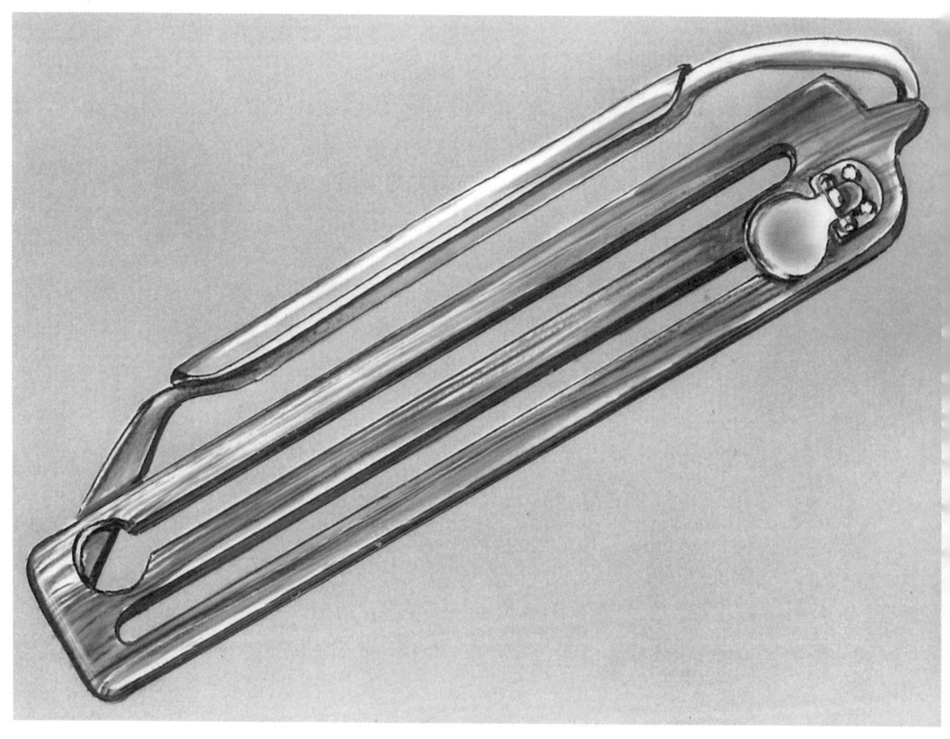

This piece of well-polished wood is about eighteen inches long with two parallel slots cut into it. At the end of each slot is a slightly larger hole with a circular hinged cover. Hanging from it is a leather strap or handle. But what was it used to carry?

*answer on page 95*

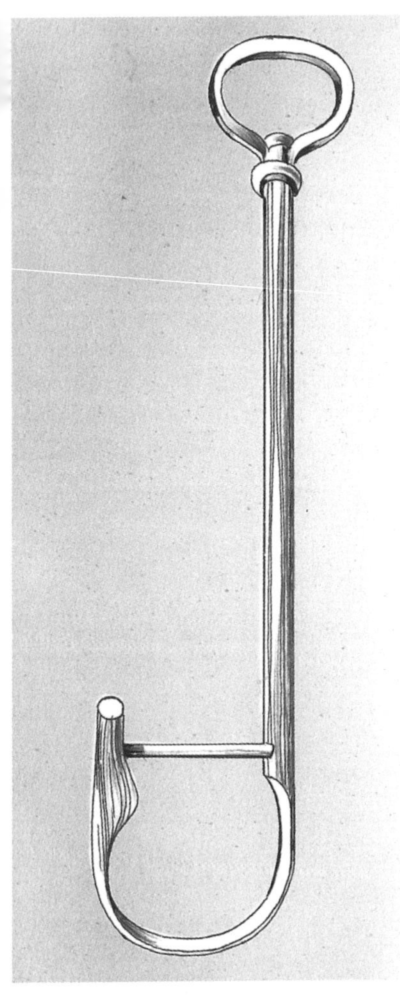

This is a very simple item and bears the marks of long usage, its wooden shaft riddled with woodworm and the metal ring pitted with rust. It was found in a barn in the Vale of York. Overall it is a little over fifteen inches long and is curved like a shepherd's crook, but that was clearly not its purpose as the hooked end is closed by a sturdy metal rod. At the other end is a ring such as might have been found on an old-fashioned key. But what on earth was it used for?

*answer on page 95*

*page 4*
It is a bottle 'boot' for extricating reluctant corks from wine bottles in the days before fancy levered corkscrews. The boot would be placed over the bottle to hold it down and then the butler would stand on the projecting metal plates to get sufficient purchase to withdraw the cork. The system also prevented spillage should the cork relent unexpectedly.

*page 5*
It is a skirt clip used by Victorian ladies to raise their trailing hems clear of muddy pavements. The skirt would be clipped between the round plates and the central ring would then be attached to a loop hanging from the lady's waist, raising it a vital couple of inches which preserved both skirt and modesty. It was sometimes known as a 'third hand' since it allowed the skirt to be raised out of the mud but still left the wearer's hands free. More elaborate versions could be used to hold the hems of ballgowns. The design pictured was patented in 1876 and was one of several types. The clips also came in useful for lady cyclists in Edwardian times — and similar items are still used by vintage bike enthusiasts.

*page 6*
The device was part of an adjustable wooden hand-drill. The drill bit was connected to a spindle which ran down the teeth on the underside of the spars on a rack and pinion system, and was probably used for drilling wooden beams *in situ*. The drill was used with the operator sitting astride the base to hold it steady while driving the bit with two handles.

*page 7*
The bar with its two swivelling clamps is a 'Plumber's Mate' which was used when soldering old-fashioned lead pipes to create a watertight joint. The bar kept the ends of the two pipes firmly in place, while the ball joints on either end of the two clamp arms allowed it to be used in even the most awkward spots.

*page 8*

The tool was used for stretching ill-fitting hats and caps for those whose heads did not conveniently fit off-the-peg sizes. The stretchers usually needed half an hour or so to do their job, and were particularly in demand after rain had shrunk caps.

*page 9*

This wooden paddle and chained dowel is a webbing stretcher, an ingeniously simple tool from the upholstery trade used in the days before rubber webbing, staple guns and foam. First, a length of webbing was fixed to one side of the chair and stretched across the area to be covered. A loop of webbing was then fed through the slot. The wooden rod was placed inside the loop and pulled taut. The groove in the end of the 'paddle' was then placed against the side of the chair and the tool levered down to get full tension on the webbing, which could then be nailed in place.

*page 10*

This object is a guillotine used until quite recently for the removal of tonsils. The metal loop was placed over the offending tonsil, which was then held by forceps while the handles were squeezed together to work the blade. Although the blade looks rather blunt, apparently it did the trick. Such operations were sometimes carried out on the kitchen table. Thirty years ago, tonsillectomies were quite common procedures — though thankfully in hospitals — and especially for children. Although such operations have now fallen out of fashion, when they are carried out a gentler procedure is used. Until about 1960 it was common for surgical instruments to be sold through pharmacies which often added their own name — that might explain the word 'Scholl' on the guillotine.

*page 11*

Dressmakers and tailors will be in no doubt that these scissors were designed for making button holes. The half-inch-long notch before the cutting edge of the blades ensured that the edge of the garment was not cut along with the button hole, as would have happened with ordinary scissors. The adjustable screw controlled how much the blades could be closed and so governed the length of the hole which was cut. Once the correct distance had been set for a particular size of button, the screw setting ensured that all the rest were cut to the same size.

*page 12*
Pipe smokers will quickly identify this as a complicated reamer for keeping pipes burning properly. Still on sale in specialist shops, the reamer is designed so the arms adjust to the shape of any pipe bowl, and can be rotated to scrape away excess carbon from the sides while still leaving the all-important carbon lining intact to provide the perfect smoke. The rounded end of the reamer protects the bottom of the pipe bowl, unlike penknives which could damage it.

*page 13*
It is a spirit measure from the days before pubs had individual optics on the bottles. Its two different sizes would be used either for different strengths of drink, or for single and double measures. The two-measure device was less likely to be misplaced, and staff could switch from one measure to the other with a flick of the wrist.

*page 14*
This mechanical marvel is an early gas-stove lighter and the ingenious forerunner of the battery-powered lighters in use in kitchens today. The spring-loaded bar would have housed a flint which rubbed against the knurled wheel to strike sparks when the trigger was pressed.

*page 15*
The pliers were once an essential part of the toolkit for repairing what are now called 'old-fashioned' typewriters. The tool was used to realign typebars which

had slipped out of place. Whether the offending letter needed to be moved up or down dictated how the typebar was fitted between the rollers.

*page 16*
This household gadget is a ‘travelling housewife’. The spindle was used to wind on different-coloured cottons, while the hollow centre held a selection of needles. The domed top would have held a thimble, while the bottom compartment could house buttons or pins. Such kits were one of the essentials in handbags sixty or more years ago, and some would have been ornately carved and decorated. The modern equivalent is the more prosaic little card of needles and thread provided in hotel bedrooms the world over.

*page 17*
It is a schoolteacher’s clicker. When the small stick is pressed against the handle and released, it makes an unpleasant noise, and, operated repeatedly by the teacher, the device was used to attract the attention of inattentive pupils. The ‘signals’, as they were known, were peculiar to Yorkshire and Lancashire, and often made from turned beech by local craftsmen.

*page 18*
This ruler is actually used for measuring lengths of cloth. The right-angle ensured that a piece of French chalk could be used to make a straight, square line ready for cutting so that no cloth was wasted. Furthermore, the markings suggest an even more specialised use: cutting fabric for aircraft wings, in the days when most airplanes had ailerons, rudders and elevators made of linen. The length of twenty-seven inches would be the width of Irish linen used, while the other markings would be used as a guide for seams.

*page 19*
The markings of ‘trot’, ‘gallop’ and ‘step out’ did indeed have military or

equestrian connotations; but not for full-sized soldiers and horses. The item was used in table-top war games which were once part of the training of Prussian army officers. This is an English copy.

*page 20*

This sturdy little machine comes from a jeweller's workshop, though it proves to have more than one use. One would be to stretch wedding rings: the ring would be placed in the appropriate-sized hole, the tapered die placed inside and the wheel turned to slowly force the die into the ring and so stretch it slightly. Another use, which must have been a far more delicate operation, was replacing cracked watchglasses. Again the replacement glass would be placed upside-down in the appropriate-sized hole and the now glassless watch laid on top of it. The wheel would then be carefully turned to force it gently into the hole. This would flex the glass and allow it to slip inside the rim of the watch. The pressure would then be released and the glass would spring back to its original size, now firmly wedged onto the watch face.

*page 21*

This domestic treasure is a rush burner, and may date from the seventeenth or eighteenth centuries. At that time there was a tax on candles, and the less well off resorted to burning rushes which had been dipped in animal fat to give them light. The rush would have been held firmly in the metal clip while it burned over the round dish. When visitors came for special occasions, the same dish might be used as a candle holder. Ironically, although they were originally used by people who could not afford candles, they are now quite valuable and collectible. How times change.

*page 22*

If you were able to turn this device over and put the blade at the top, its use would become more apparent as a nineteenth-century wick trimmer and cutter for paraffin lamps. A catalogue from a London company, Silber & Flemming, dated 1883, includes a very similar item.

*page 23*
The tool was used by hatmakers to provide the finished shape and sheen to headgear. This explains the high polish on the outer face while the inner one, which was never used, remained rough and unfinished. The intriguing lip along one edge was used to create the crisp angle between the crown and the brim. A less official use was for giving cheeky apprentices a sharp tap, but the wielder had to be careful — too hefty a swipe with one of the heavier irons could inflict serious damage.

*page 24*
This is a fid, though perhaps it would be better known to lovers of old seafaring films in its metal version, a marlin spike. The spike, like its much smaller cousin found on Boy Scouts' penknives, would have been used to open up the twists in ropes for joining and splicing. Sizes vary: bigger ships use bigger ropes, which in turn need bigger fids to open them up.

*page 25*
This unusual knife will prove no problem to those who have worked in science laboratories. It is a tool used to sharpen the metal tubes which bored holes in corks. The holes were needed to allow glass tubes to pass through the corks sealing test-tubes and vessels. But the borers — metal tubes with sharpened rims made of soft metal, such as brass — quickly became blunt with use. The cone was inserted into the end of the tube of the borer and the blade held down so that, as the borer was twisted, a thin shaving was taken off the edge, leaving it sharp again. Sets of borers might run to ten or more in various diameters from 3mm to a centimetre, but, because the nose cone of the sharpener could be pushed into any size of borer, a single sharpener worked for all sizes.

*page 26*

This complex contraption is a photographer's magnesium lamp. Many will have seen film of the primitive 'flash guns' used by early photographers who set fire to magnesium powder to create a brief, bright light. Our device is an even earlier, if less spectacular model, possibly dating from the 1860s. Magnesium ribbon, which burned with a bright flame, was stored in the drum at the bottom and then fed through to the tube above the reflector dish. It was then set alight to create a bright light. Fresh ribbon could be fed through the reflector by turning the rollers. Slightly more sophisticated versions had a system for giving preset amounts of ribbon for any given exposure. While the light was undoubtedly bright, the white 'smoke' of magnesium was sometimes overpowering and no small fire hazard.

*page 27*

It is a 'bug viewer'. The specimen to be examined would be impaled on the spike and studied in detail via the tiny lens. The item dates probably from Victorian times when gentlemen amateurs took a keen interest in science or, as it was then termed, 'Natural Philosophy'. A Dutch optician and botanist, Anton van Leeuwenhoek, had developed a high-magnification device using a single lens, but later models incorporated two lenses and took on the shape still known today.

*page 28*

It is a traveller's lock. The idea was that you slotted the flat plate into the lock in the door frame, and then closed the door and slotted the pin through the hole closest to the door to stop it being opened. Though it might have stopped a sneak thief, whether it would have stopped a determined intruder is debatable. Years ago, such devices were designed to guard young ladies, and were bought by mothers for their daughters travelling away from home for the first time to protect their virtue.

*page 29*

It is a mechanical burglar alarm, though slightly more sophisticated than the one of page 28. The alarm was wound up and the hook slipped over a handy doorknob or bracket. The weight at the end of the chain was balanced on the window frame or even the doorknob itself. If anyone tried to enter, the weight slipped off and triggered the alarm. It looks very heavy and convoluted, but the basic idea is still around today in the battery-powered versions used by backpackers the world over.

*page 30*

An almost identical version of this stands in the Wimbledon Tennis Museum. It is a juice squeezer and used to provide refreshing drinks for players between games. The squeezer is late Victorian or early Edwardian, and the rings at either side would have been used to hold tumblers. Half an orange, or lemon, would be placed in the cup, and the press operated by the screw of the threaded handle. The juice would then have drained through the holes into the tumblers or a jug placed in the depression underneath. What an elegant way to prepare drinks.

*page 31*

This is the delightfully titled Crazy Daisy Winder, used in embroidery. The knob is turned to make the rods protrude from the centre and embroidery thread is then woven over the spokes, criss-crossing the centre to make a daisy pattern before the thread is tied off in the centre. The knob is then turned to retract the spokes, allowing the finished 'daisy' to be slipped off. Once several daisies have been produced, they can be linked to create whatever shape is required.

*page 32*

It is a primitive tin-opener. The point would be stabbed into the centre of the tin and then pushed down until the flanges fitted over the rim and the sharp blade could be dragged round to open the can. Because the openers were dependent on brute force, they were difficult to use and were quickly superseded by more advanced designs — though ex-soldiers will recall using them as army issue. They do have one advantage: because the blades were doubled-sided, they could be used equally easily by left- or right-handed cooks.

*page 33*

This, too, is an early can opener, possibly late Victorian. The blade is stabbed through the tin lid and the peg used as a fulcrum to open the tin completely. There is quite an art to using it, as it leaves a ragged edge in the top of the tin.

*page 34*

Veteran pipe smokers will identify this as a contraption for cutting up twist tobacco. The twist, which resembled a thick stick of liquorice, was cut to the length of the tube with the base plate wound down. The top was then turned to cut thin slices of tobacco. As the top was turned, the spindle on the plate kept the next slice pushed to the top. Those without an automatic slicer would have had to use a sharp penknife: it was an art to hold the plug in one hand, the knife in the other and manage to catch the slices of plug for rubbing in the palm of the smoker's hand. No wonder ready-rubbed tobacco became more popular.

*page 35*

The slimline device will be an easy target for those with military experience, as it is a compass for setting an artillery piece. The compass was temporarily attached to the gun to ensure that north on the gun barrel was correctly aligned before bearings were taken on the target. Because the gun would already have been roughly aligned, the 'Director' compass needed to show only a few degrees either side of north. The Director may seem to be on a large scale but it needed to be read very accurately. If a shell was being fired over several miles, a mistake of only a fraction of a degree in the aiming would mean it landed a long way off target.

*page 36*
This ring and chain device will bring back memories for postal workers who had to deliver floods of Christmas cards, often on snow and ice. It would have been one of a pair issued to postmen as a safety precaution in wintry conditions. The rubber ring was fitted over the welt of the boot or shoe, with the chains passed under the foot to give a firm grip.

*page 37*
It is actually a table-top match dispenser. Each 'petal' of the daisy wheel contained one or more matches, which were stored safely out of harm's way. When one was needed, the lid was flipped open and a match torn out. Once a section of matches had been used, the knob on top of the box was turned to produce a fresh section. The match was then struck on the roughened top of the box — hence the red 'inlay' from all those striking match heads.

*page 38*
This fiercesome-looking object has quite a sweet application. It is a pair of sugar nippers. In the days before sugar arrived finely granulated in two-pound bags, it was sold in slabs, and the nippers were used to break it up into more genteel lumps for the tea table or for cooking. The blades did not need to be sharpened because the sugar was brittle, although sharp blades were needed if the sugar came in cone form which could be almost three feet high. The nippers were versatile, and could be used for breaking up other foodstuffs such as salt or slabs of toffee.

*page 39*
It is a herb chopper, and was ideally suited for cutting herbs very finely for mint or parsley sauces. It was also safe to operate, and so could be by young children. Similar ones are still in use today, which just goes to show that some gadgets can't be improved upon.

*page 40*
This particular spoon-shaped device is a refugee from the Indian Raj, where it had been used for drinking tea which was brewed in the cup and then sucked up through the mouthpiece of the spoon which strained out the tea leaves. Its origin, however, is likely to be a little further west. In Argentina the spoon is known as a *bombilla* and is used to drink *Yerba Mate*, which is brewed from an infusion of leaves. It would have originally come with a teacup-sized gourd.

*page 41*
It might look like a fancy butter knife, but in fact its use was on the writing desk rather than the tea table. The hooked end was used to scratch out mistakes, much in the way a rubber eraser is used today. The rounded handle was then used to smooth the roughened paper back into place so the new figure could be entered. Such knives would have been used in accounts offices to scrub out mistakes in ledgers. Needless to say, the paper used in the ledgers had to be fairly robust to stand up to such treatment: some auditors frowned on the practice, preferring to see the mistake crossed out and corrected.

*page 42*
These clippers date from the beginning of the twentieth century and were used to 'set' hand-saws. The saw teeth were placed between the screws on the clippers, which were then adjusted to give the correct amount of 'set'. Each alternate tooth was then adjusted before the saw was turned round and the remainder finished off.

*page 43*
This is a device for sharpening circular saws (as against the hand-saw set shown on page 42). The tooth on the circular saw is inserted into the appropriate slot for the thickness of blade and the sliding arms are set at the extent of set required, ie fine or coarse. The handle is pressed downwards until the gauge

comes to rest on the blade body; every alternate tooth is set in this way, and then the opposite teeth are set from the other side of the blade. The circle at the top of the slot ensures that the newly sharpened tooth edge is not damaged.

*page 44*
It is a muzzle designed to prevent unwanted suckling by calves or young heifers. The muzzle was fitted to the head of the young animal so that, whenever it tried to suckle, the spikes prodded the cow's udders, making it move away from the calf. Problems also occurred when young heifers were introduced to the dairy herd to get them used to the hurly burly of milking time, even though they were not producing milk themselves. They could try to suckle older cows that had milk; but not even the most maternal cow would tolerate one of these muzzles for long.

*page 45*
It is a clamping tool used in harvesting honey from beehives. In the days of straw bee-skeps, the combs had to be cut out, and were put in a muslin 'poke' and hung from a beam. The clamp would be fixed around the top of the bag and slowly lowered to force the honey through the muslin to be caught in a basin underneath.

*page 46*
Although many will agree on the use of this item, they may well differ on the name. In Kent it is known as a thistle spudder, a dockweed spud and a thistle lifter. Just as a rose by any other name ... so with a weed extractor, specifically one for single large-rooted plants. It works by the forked tip being driven into the ground alongside the offending plant and then levered backwards using the curled metal piece as a fulcrum, so that the weed is removed, tap root and all.

*page 47*
It is a 'twitch', used to restrain recalcitrant horses while they were attended to by vets or farriers. The loop of leather was slipped over the horse's upper lip and

the stick twisted to tighten it. The effect, apparently, was near miraculous at bringing the horse under control. Attaching the twitch sounded perilous but seemingly was easily done once the knack was learned.

*page 48*
This device is used to make a hole in the end of cigars. Usually, cigar cutters remove the end of the cigar to allow it to be smoked, but these 'scissors' allowed the end to be left intact. Instead of removing the end, the spike was used to pierce the side of the cigar close to the end.

*page 49*
They are forceps used to help with difficult lambings. Ewes can usually be left to produce their youngsters themselves, but every shepherd also had to know how to cope with difficult births such as when the lamb faces the wrong way. Either end of the forceps could be used, depending on the problem, while the jointed hook, blunted to avoid damage to the ewe, could be used to pull stray limbs into position to make it easier for the lamb to be born.

*page 50*
This clip was probably used for leading bulls around the farm. The 'snaffler' would be clipped into the bull's nose and a bull staff would then be attached to the smaller ring so that the animal could, theoretically, be led fairly docilely thanks to the pressure on its tender nose. A smaller clip was occasionally used for pigs. Particularly ferocious bulls were sometimes fitted with permanent nose rings, from which a heavy block of wood dangled to impede the animal if it tried to chase farmworkers. How the bull was persuaded to stand still long enough to have the clip inserted in the first place is another mystery.

*page 51*
They are pig ringers. Curved pieces of wire with two sharp ends were fitted into

the jaws of the pliers and then nipped closed through pigs' snouts to deter them from uprooting grass in fields. But why two pairs of pincers? The larger pair of jaws could have been used to insert the ring initially and the smaller set used to nip the ring tight. Another explanation is that the different-sized jaws were for different-sized rings. But merely looking at the needle-sharp rings is enough to make the eyes water.

*page 52*
This item is a charcoal torch or cage used during the Victorian age for burning off old paint in the days before blowlamps. As with more modern variations, the torch was held up to the surface to soften the paint which could then be scraped away easily. Presumably, then as now, the trick was to melt the paint without setting fire to the wood beneath. The charcoal cages were superseded in the late nineteenth century by more efficient and more elaborate paraffin- and petrol-burning lamps.

*page 53*
Picture, if you will, a crossroads. At the centre stands an organ, while on each of the four streets stands a collector, each armed with a tin like this one. A coin is placed in the tin and the collectors rattle them in time to the music, so providing both an accompaniment to the music and an incentive to passers-by to drop more coins in the collecting box. This example is similar to those still used by Dutch organ operators, and may also have been used by troupes of morris dancers or at plough stots events in country villages.

*page 54*
The object was known as a 'butler' or 'poor man's valet' (though descriptions vary) and had various uses. The spike at the top would have held a watch chain and fob when it was not needed, while the tray at the bottom was for loose change. It could also have been used to keep freshly starched collars tidy in the

days when men's shirts came with detachable collars. The tray at the bottom would then be used to hold the special studs which attached the collars to the shirt.

*page 55*
It is a Victorian flycatcher. A sweet liquid was placed in the circular trough which ran around the inside of the base of the jar, and this attracted the insects which flew in through the large hole in the base. Once inside, they found themselves unable to escape, and eventually fell into the liquid and drowned. Less elegant home-made versions were often created from old jamjars half filled with water.

*page 56*
It is a quilting attachment for a sewing machine. The stem of the quilter passes through an eye in the foot of the sewing machine, which holds the needle and thread, and is set to whatever distance is required by adjusting the rod, which is then fixed in place with a screw. The foot of the quilter runs along the previous line of stitching to ensure a neat even spacing between the lines.

*page 57*
Old soldiers will recognise this as a standard army-issue brass oil bottle which was part of the cleaning kit for the Short Magazine Lee Enfield 303 rifle used by British and Commonwealth troops in both world wars. The butt plate of the rifle had a circular lid which gave access to a tube where the entire kit of oil bottle, pull-through and roll of flannelette could be kept.

*page 58*
This tool would have been used by wheelwrights repairing horse-drawn waggons, and was one of a wealth of strange-looking but very effective tools (some of which are also to be found in this book) used in the complicated business of

constructing wooden wheels. The finished wheel was firmly clamped together by the iron tyre, which was heated over a fire until it glowed red and expanded, and then slipped over the wheel so that it contracted and gripped everything together, but the other components were also held in a tension of their own. Part of this was achieved by the spokes being splayed out at a slightly greater angle than the slots they fitted into in the outer rim or felloe. That meant that, when the wheel was complete, the natural springiness of the spokes helped to hold them in place. First, however, the spokes had to be pulled closer together to slip them into the slots in the felloes, which is where our clamp comes in. The hook was fixed over one spoke and the swivelling handle slipped behind the adjoining one, and then the wheelwright pulled, using the leverage to nip the spokes closer together so that section of rim could be fitted.

page *59*
Like the one on page 58, this item would also have been in common use among blacksmiths and wheelwrights. It is a rim clamp used during the making or repair of wagon wheels. Once the hub had been made, the spokes were fastened into it before the rim was built up in short curved sections, known as felloes. The ring on our device would be hooked over the hub, and then the clamp tightened to force the felloes neatly into place and make sure everything fitted neatly — though some chaps just used a hammer.

*page 60*
A pair of these objects were used by telephone engineers to climb wooden telegraph posts. Each was fitted to the foot like a stirrup: the shorter arm fitted under the boot, while the longer arm was strapped tightly to the inside of the climber's calf, using a thigh strap missing from our example. This left the small spike on the inside of the instep. With one on each foot, the engineer would stamp the spike into the wood of the pole and quickly shin up it without the need for a ladder.

*page 61*

This was a vital tool for foresters, lumberjacks and even teams laying railway lines. The head, pictured, would have been fitted with a handle, perhaps six feet or more long. The spike was stabbed into the log to be manhandled and the pivoting hook would catch onto the side of the trunk, gripping it firmly and allowing it to be moved without too much risk to life or limb.

*page 62*

It is a wartime device for picking up incendiary bombs before disposing of them in a bucket of sand. Such bomb-disposal equipment has since been put to some ingenious uses. To clean out gullies on a farm, the open scoop was pushed into the mud, then the lid closed to stop the debris falling back into the water as it was pulled upwards. It has also come in handy in the autumn as a leaf collector.

*page 63*

This spiked horror is not an instrument of torture after all, but a comb used for 'scutching' straw to prepare it for use in thatching. Loose leaves, chaff and even stray grain had to be removed before the straw could form a waterproof barrier. Rogue grains were a particular problem as, once they became wet, they could start to sprout, spoiling not only the look of the roof but its efficiency. The sheaf was grasped at the base and pulled through the comb, which removed the unwanted bits and left the stalks clean and straight.

*page 64*

This intriguing-looking item is a scraper used after exercise when horses have to be cooled down. The animal is first hosed down, and then the excess water and dust removed by scraping the curved blade down its flanks. Sometimes a handful of straw would be used by the stable boy or girl to finish things off. Straw was also put under the stable rug to allow air to get to the animal's back and speed up the drying process.

*page 65*
It is a router used when grooves of various depths or widths had to be cut. Such routers were used for making all kinds of housing joints — for example by craftsmen making staircases, with different widths being used for treads and risers — but have since been superseded by electrical tools. It is doubtful, however, if the modern versions rejoice in the nickname for our antique — an owd granny's tooth. Another name for it is a rabbit knife, although this could be a corruption of 'rebate knife', again suggesting the knife was used for cutting grooves in wood, with the changeable blades giving a variety of depths and widths.

*page 66*
This object has been described, picturesquely, as a 'corkwhopperiner' and as a reverse corkscrew. Basically, it was used to put corks in wine bottles. The corks were softened in hot water before being placed in the middle of the opened levers. These were then closed tightly shut to squeeze the cork. The plunger then pushed the cork tightly into the neck of the bottle, where it promptly expanded to create the seal. A more modern version of this splendid brass corker can still be bought in wine making shops.

*page 67*
It is for splitting the drive chains of bikes and motorcycles, and would push out the riveted pins which would be replaced by a split link or two, enabling the chain to be shortened or extended. Exposed chains meant plenty of wear and tear, and so plenty of repairs. A link extractor was therefore a cyclist's most valuable tool.

*page 68*
They are pliers used to nip closed the seal on a full milk churn. A thin piece of wire was looped through a hole in the churn's lid and through a ring fastened

to its neck. The wire was then secured with a lead seal, which was nipped into place with these pliers.

*page 69*
It was known as a wimble, and was used to wind stems of corn into a short rope or bond to tie sheaves of corn. During harvest, the edges of the field would be cut first, and it was these stems which were woven together to form the bonds before the binder went in to gather the main crop.

*page 70*
It is a sliding bevel, used by generations of joiners and carpenters, builders and wheelwrights. This particular one is an outsize model which may well have been used to mark out large sheets of plywood or hardboard, or to mark out and check the angles of roof timbers, for example. The bevel was used either to transfer an angle from a drawing to wood or to copy it from one piece to another. It is laid against the drawing or guide piece and the screw loosened to allow the arm to move. Once it has been set at the correct place the screw is tightened to hold it in position so that it can be transferred to the wood to be cut.

*page 71*
It is an adjustable double plane used by basket makers to prepare willow rods. To achieve an even finish, the pliable rods were passed between the blades to produce a uniform size. The same tool could also be used to peel away the bark on some rods to reveal the paler wood beneath if a patterned effect was required.

*page 72*
The timer was used to take patients' pulses. The count was taken over half a minute and then doubled to arrive at the final figure. These 'pulseometers' were essential pieces of equipment after the Second World War when watches with

second hands were virtually unobtainable. There were different models which ran for 15, 30 and 60 seconds, with the full minute version being the most accurate.

*page 73*
It is a hay spade, used for cutting up stacks into bales. This elaborate version is likely to have belonged to a specialist contractor rather than a farmer. Farms with big acreages of hay would sell their surplus to specialist dealers who had to cut up the stack before it could be carried away. They used a special rod to pluck hay from the centre of a sack to assess its quality and, if satisfied, fix a price. They then cut it up using hay spades which had heart shaped blades and extra wide handles so the user could get a firm purchase. Once cut the bales were bound with twine for transport.

*page 74*
This rustic contraption is a game carrier used to carry a number of birds during or after the shoot. It worked by slotting the bird's head through the large hole and then sliding it along the slot. According to the size of the carrier, a number of birds could be carried easily by one person with the strap being used either as a handle or slipped over the shoulder.

*page 75*
This device was used for fashioning straw ropes during haytime. The hook was fastened to the farmworker's belt with a short piece of twine to keep it handy. Then, when needed, the straw was fixed through the hook and the shaft twisted to create the rope.

A catalogue of all Dalesman magazines, books, calendars and videos/DVDs can be obtained from

Country Publications Ltd
The Water Mill
Broughton Hall
Skipton
North Yorkshire
BD23 3AG
UK

*Tel:* (+44) 01756 701033
*Email:* sales@dalesman.co.uk

*Order online at*
www.dalesman.co.uk